Women and Mental Health
New Directions for Change

Women and Mental Health
New Directions for Change

Carol T. Mowbray, PhD, Susan Lanir, MA,
and Marilyn Hulce, MSW, ACSW
Editors

The Haworth Press
New York • London

Paperback edition, 1986.

Women and Mental Health: New Directions for Change has also been published as *Women & Therapy,* Volume 3, Numbers 3/4, Fall/Winter 1984.

The Haworth Press, Inc., 28 East 22 Street, New York, NY 10010-6194
EUROSPAN/Haworth, 3 Henrietta Street, London WC2E 8LU England

Library of Congress Cataloging in Publication Data
Main entry under title:

Women and mental health.

   "Has also been published as Women & therapy, volume 3, numbers 3/4, fall/winter 1984"—T.p. verso.
   Bibliography: p.
   1. Women—Mental health services. 2. Women—Mental health. 3. Sexism in mental health services. I. Mowbray, Carol T. II. Lanir, Susan. III. Hulce, Marilyn.
RC451.4.W6W6455   1984   362.2'088042   84-19228
ISBN 0-86656-331-8
ISBN 0-86656-437-3 (pbk.)

Women and Mental Health
New Directions for Change

Women & Therapy
Volume 3, Numbers 3/4

CONTENTS

Foreword

The feminist quarterly, *Women & Therapy,* is proud to present this special double issue (volume 3, numbers 3/4) which is written by the Women's Task Force of the Department of Mental Health in the State of Michigan. The Task Force is composed of women health professionals who are aware of sexism in the mental health services provided by the State and have taken action to change the biased treatment of women. Their findings are based on public hearings and a thorough review of relevant literature.

Women & Therapy supports the revamping of public mental health services so that the traditional patriarchal view no longer prevails, a view which typically defines the woman as "the patient" and "the problem." We need a feminist perspective which takes into account the specific and different needs of women and men. What is commonly labelled "pathology" in women patients in state agencies is often the woman's desperate response to highly stressful situations like loss of financial support, physical abuse, pregnancy, and marital problems. Professionally led problem-solving support groups can effectively deal with many of the problems facing women which are traditionally treated by medication and/or hospitalization. The Women's Task Force makes specific recommendations along these lines.

We are interested to hear about your experiences, as readers, to this study. And we continue to welcome women to submit articles relevant to feminism and psychotherapy. Send letters and manuscripts to: Betts Collett, Editor, 435 Split Rock Road, Syosset, NY 11791.

A special thanks to Carol Mowbray of the Women's Task Force for her leadership in preparing this study for publication.

In sisterhood,
Betts Collett

Introduction

The existence of sex differences in mental health problems and sexist treatment by mental health agencies is no secret. Nor is it recent news. The husband who tried to "gaslight"* and inappropriately institutionalize his wife was a frequent theme of early 20th century novels and old movies. Phyllis Chesler, in *Women and Madness* (1973), was the first to bring this topic to public attention and she did so in a startling exposé. That was more than a decade ago. Since then, a host of changes have occurred in the women's movement. Yet, for those of us who work in the mental health system, many of the abuses which Chesler revealed have not changed! Inappropriate admissions, diagnostic sexism, overmedication, exploitation, biases in wellness concepts—these things are all still with us.

Our perception of the problems of sexism first caused us to establish a Women's Task Force in our state mental health agency. After an extensive search for appropriate members, we identified twelve women from Michigan employed in a variety of mental health settings, who represented the major professional mental health disciplines, providing clinical, administrative, and clerical services. When the Task Force began to work, we were fortunate to have Jean Baker Miller, the feminist psychiatrist who directs the Stone Center for Developmental Services at Wellesley College, assist us in formulating our course of action. She advised us to take a broad sweep of the issues and to focus on system change. She also shared information on change efforts that have been successful.

Once the Task Force was established, we began holding public hearings on women's mental health problems and their treatment. Topics as diverse as women living alone, rural women, minority women, women and substance abuse, and many, many more were addressed. The results of the public forums confirmed our percep-

---

*In the 1930s movie, *"Gaslight,"* Charles Boyer schemed to gain control over the fortune of his wife, Ingrid Bergman, by making her think she was crazy through various devious actions. One tactic was turning down all the gaslights and telling her *she* had done it.

tions of women's problems in treatment. Furthermore, we were alarmed at the lack of consciousness displayed by many mental health professionals over what, to us, were blatant and biased sex differences. For example, one of our public forums focused on treatment of women in inpatient psychiatric facilities. To locate presenters for the forum, we consulted numerous clinical directors in psychiatric hospitals. Half of this group of male psychiatrists staunchly *denied* that there were *any* sex differences in mental health problems or treatment. The other half were more open, indicating that the possibility of sex differences had never occurred to them, but they would consult their staff. After talking to their nursing staff, they did inform us that, "Yes, indeed, we had an issue. Sex differences did exist!" Needless to say, the speakers for this public forum were the nurses—*not* the clinical directors!

Based on our information-gathering on this topic over the last three years, we feel a new approach is needed. It is time for concerned mental health professionals—therapists and administrators—to take responsible action. The solutions to the problems are evident—they *must* be acted on for change to occur. The pervasive extent and overwhelming nature of the problems must be recognized; and a general recognition is not enough. More importantly, the commitment must be made to create change—to advocate for and carry out specific activities which *will* produce improvements.

We have produced *Women and Mental Health: New Directions for Change,* to contribute to these change efforts. The focus is twofold. First,

—TO PRESENT THE MOST RELEVANT, UP-TO-DATE DATA AND FACTUAL EVIDENCE ON WOMEN'S MENTAL HEALTH PROBLEMS, CAUSES, AND TREATMENT.

Much of what is reported in the popular literature and in journal articles is one-sided and does not present an accurate, overall picture of what we know and where the gaps are. Literature tends to get summarized from the perspective of the author to make his/her point. Unfortunately, the points that get published are *rarely* feminist ones. Thus, for each of the major topics we address, the editors have prepared a concise yet readable overview of the evidence—the facts—which have been written, reported and researched. We feel that only with such a factual basis behind them can feminist change agents feasibly move forward.

In contrast to the sections on evidence, we also present "Perspectives''—the individual views of prominent female scholars and practitioners concerning the problem from their own experiential backgrounds.

The second focus is:

—TO PRESENT RECOMMENDED CHANGES AND ALTER-NATIVES FOR IMPROVING PREVENTION AND TREAT-MENT OF WOMEN'S MENTAL HEALTH PROBLEMS.

The activities of the Women's Task Force have gone beyond mere problem identification. We have also identified viable solutions, effective alternatives, and change ingredients—as specifically as possible. Major sections of this work describe the changes which can be undertaken. We also present recommendations for action—addressed to mental health administrators, clinicians, and clients themselves. If these changed practices can be undertaken, we are confident that improvements in women's mental health *can* occur.

The chapters in *Women and Mental Health* represent the combined efforts of the editors in conducting literature reviews, the presenters at our public forums in preparing their remarks for publication, clinicians and consumers in contributing case studies, and the Women's Task Force in formulating strategies for recommended change.

The experience of amassing the information for this book and its literary production has been positive and enlightening for us and, we believe, for the clients we serve. *Women and Mental Health* is being published with the belief that it will be as beneficial to our readers.

The Editors

SECTION 1:
SEX DIFFERENCES IN WOMEN'S MENTAL HEALTH PROBLEMS AND THEIR CAUSES: THE EVIDENCE

OVERVIEW

How would you answer the following questions:

Are there sex differences in mental health problems? Yes or No?
Who has more mental health problems? Women or men?

If given this quiz, most people would probably correctly respond "yes" to the first question, since sex differences are reported in almost every area! Most would probably also correctly guess "women" as the answer to the second question. However, few people would correctly identify the significant extent to which women outnumber men not only in self-reports of psychiatric symptoms but also in diagnostic interview measures and in utilization of mental health services. And even fewer people would be aware of the complexity of this sex difference—sex interacts with many other demographic variables in relationship to mental health problems.

This chapter gives an overview of sex differences in mental health, as measured by a multiplicity of indicators, and the major theoretical explanations to account for these results. In order to understand more thoroughly the problems women have in receiving appropriate mental health treatment, we must begin with a basic knowledge of the research evidence on the extent and type of mental health problems women have and some explanations as to why they have these problems.

SEX DIFFERENCES IN PREVALENCE

The degree of mental disturbance in the population is difficult, if not impossible, to estimate because of differing criteria and methods. However, with startling consistency, many studies researching sex differences in mental health problems have produced similar results: the female population has a higher percentage of "mentally ill" individuals than does the male population (Guttentag, 1980; Gove, 1979).

Consistent and significant sex differences have also been documented in the utilization of mental health services. Women, especially older women, outnumber men in diagnoses of schizophrenia and in depression in all age categories (Weissman and Klerman, 1979; Guttentag, 1980; Deming, 1968; Freedman et al., 1972; Rosenthal, 1970).

One often-hypothesized explanation for these sex differences is simply that women complain more than men. However, a recent national survey (Veroff et al., 1981) found that when asked about jobs, men are more unhappy and worry *more* than women do; women worry more about their children and their family's health. These results and others (Gove, 1979; Weissman and Klerman, 1979) argue against sex differences being solely attributable to response style.

The Special Subpanel on the Mental Health of Women from the President's Commission on Mental Health summed up the differences as follows:

> Women constitute 51 percent of the population, and the evidence suggests that they are overrepresented among the mentally ill. Women have more negative images of themselves than do men (Gove and Tudor, 1973), and population surveys of nonpatients show that women report more personal discomfort as well as

symptoms consistent with mental illness twice as frequently as do men (Gove and Tudor, 1973). . . . The information on first admissions to mental hospitals, psychiatric treatment in general hospitals, psychiatric outpatient clinics, private outpatient psychiatric care, the practices of general physicians, and community surveys all indicate that more women than men are mentally ill (Gove and Tudor, 1973). (Subpanel, 1978, p. 316)

What should we deduce from this definitive statement? Besides the typically inferred female genetic ''weaknesses'' in math abilities, logical thinking and achievement motivation, should we now add mental health problems to the list? Obviously not. Instead, we concur with the conclusions from a recent, large-scale, national survey (Veroff et al., 1981):

Women are more demoralized than men. . .women, more than men, report difficulties in their daily lives. . . women finding life more problematic than men.

. . .sex differences in subjective mental health are not merely a function of men's relative reluctance to see themselves as problematic and/or to report difficulties to a strange interviewer. Instead, we interpret the patterns of results as indicating that women's life situations confront them with experiences which put them in a more vulnerable position than men, a position that engenders psychological difficulties. (pp. 373-4)

THEORIES OF SEX DIFFERENCES IN MENTAL ILLNESS

Ever since sex differences have been identified, a rich array of theories have arisen to explain them. Our review encompasses psychoanalytic, biological/genetic and sociocultural approaches.

Most disheartening to feminists and, luckily, easiest to dismiss, are explanations based on *psychoanalytic theory.* According to Freudian theory, adult women are characterized by narcissism, masochism, low self-esteem, dependency, and inhibited hostility as a consequence of the young girl's special resolution of the Oedipal complex. Since depression corresponds to difficulties in close relationships, early childhood deprivation, excessive guilt, dependency, and a tendency to turn hostility inward, women are seen as more vulnerable to depression than men because of their early life experiences and "typical" personality characteristics. Simply stated, the psychoanalytic explanation suggests that characteristics and life experiences of persons prone to depression are *like* the traits and experiences typical of women. Empirical data to support this theory is almost nil. Women's pervasive unhappiness became a subject of psychotherapy in an attempt to explain it through psychological rather than social status differences, but clinical theory has never accurately and realistically addressed women's development and conflict (Hare-Mustin, 1983).

More engrained in current mythologies are the *biological/genetic theories* of sex differences. It is true that research has established a genetic basis for mental illness: close relatives of depressives have higher rates of depression. In terms of sex differences, however, the results are more complex (Weissman and Klerman, 1979), for example, female, but not male twins are more likely to develop schizophrenia (Wahl, 1976). Explanations for such sex differences would have to link genetic transmission of mental illness to the "X" chromosome. This evidence is lacking and research in this area is still quite limited.

Biological theories propose that the female reproductive cycle and endocrine system make women more susceptible to mental illness. Although correlations have been made between different phases of the menstrual cycle and symptoms of depression, in review, the methodological problems in these studies preclude reliable conclusions (Sommer, 1973; Parlee, 1972; Weissman and Klerman, 1979). The fact that the postpartum period, involving a very significant hormonal shift in a woman's body, has been associated with psychiatric disorders and that pregnant women are *less* likely to be affected by emotional disturbances (especially depression), has also suggested that hormones are related to mood changes and emotional states (Paffenbarger and McCabe, 1966). However, while these relationships are well-established, the specific endocrine mechanism involved, if any, is not. Emotional changes associated with menopause have also been used to establish a biological basis for depression. Contrary to popular belief, however, research shows there *are no* significant links between menopause and depression (Klerman and Weissman, 1980). Overall, the relationship between changes in mood states or depression and specific hormones in females is weak and inconsistent (Weissman and Klerman, 1979). A biological basis alone is not sufficient to explain sex differences in depression.

In contrast to the previous theories, a *sociocultural* approach emphasizes stress factors in the woman's environment which adversely affect mental health such as: women's socialization, lowered social status, sex discrimination, stereotypic biases, and discrepancies between rising expectations and actuality.

A woman's socialization engrains in her prevailing patriarchal attitudes and norms regarding her "appropriate" role. These role expectations may make women particularly vulnerable to mental "unhealth." Women are taught to accept certain behaviors as part of their role: to be at the service of others, avoid aggressiveness and refrain from any display of anger or hostility. Women have a more negative orientation toward themselves than do men; and women more than men judge their shortcomings on the basis of deeper, more individuated qualities and hold more internal aspirations for identity (Veroff et al., 1981), implying women "may rely on others for confirmation of their adequacy more than men do" (p. 128). One national survey found striking sex differences in women's greater difficulties forging their own identities. Women of every age described the same dilemma: "How do I stop trying so hard to please others and begin to validate myself?"

> . . .the most troubled women's written descriptions of how they handle crises and transitions indicate that they are all too ready to assume personal responsibility for the husband who cannot hold a job, the child who is not getting along in school, the alcoholic father, the ill-tempered employer. And when their friends become

disloyal or their bosses do not give them promotions,
they think it must be because of something they have
done. . . The paradox is that the same low-well-being
women seldom take responsibility—or credit—for the
good things. (Sheehy, 1981, p. 94)

In childhood, boys are under more pressure than girls.
They operate within a narrower range of appropriate behavior and experience more stringent sex role expectations.
However, beginning in adolescence (age 15 and up), females experience more stress as well as mental health problems from the need to abandon masculine activities (like
achievement), from increased pressure to adopt the feminine role, and from greater awareness of males' favored
status (Gove, 1979). When a woman deviates from the prescribed feminine sex-role, society and its mental health professionals may question her so-called femininity and, ultimately, her mental health.

Another theorized aspect of female socialization is
"learned helplessness"—the gradual loss or non-develop-
ment of a sense of mastery, control or autonomy based on a
continued lack of reinforcement between one's actions and
outcomes. Researchers have established that continual exposure to events which are outside of an individual's control
affects that individual's ability to perceive a relationship between his/her action and its consequences, reducing the
subsequent motivation to act on his/her environment. When
uncontrollable events are aversive, considerable emotional
disruption often results. Researchers have easily condi-
tioned helplessness in animals and humans through labora-
tory experiments (Bloom, 1979). In real life, the learned
helplessness of women can result from often being in situations they cannot control, as well as from the realism that
exerting control is contrary to the feminine role. Feelings of
loss of autonomy, control and self-direction arise from
learned helplessness and depression may result. Without
any control, how can a woman help but wonder, "Is there
something wrong with *me?*" She will accept responsibility
for her pathology (whether real or perceived) when it is not
justified. Through these mechanisms, women's socialization may account for emotional problems and predispose
women to mental "unhealth," especially depression.

Women's second class citizenship also has distinct implications for their mental health and treatment. Very few women are in positions of power. Even when women work, they have lower status than men (Gove, 1979). This gives them not only an obvious sense of powerlessness, but also limits the likelihood of social or political change for their benefit. The "ungratifying, restrictive, almost demeaning role that women play in modern society is a source of emotional problems" (Gove and Tudor, 1973), and so contributes to the differences in mental illness and the treatment provided the sexes.

Discrimination is also a significant factor, and can lead to dependency on others, low aspirations and, ultimately, clinical depression. In the provision of certain mental health services, as well as in the employment, social and political spheres, discrimination against women has been documented. Since 1940, there has been a consistent decline in the status of women compared to men (Gove, 1979). Discrimination, when personalized, can influence a woman's mental health in various ways through a questioning of one's self-worth. Also, in experiencing inequities in life situations—such as in employment—the sense of mastery is lost. A person locked in an inferior position cannot help but think and feel powerless. Depression may be a natural response to these conditions.

The fact that a number of demographic factors relate strongly to mental health problems in women lends support to sociocultural explanations: larger families, lower educational and economic status, single parenting, and lack of a supporting relationship are all significant risk factors for women (Brown et al., 1975; Soloman and Bromet, 1982; Costello, 1982; Pearlin, 1975; Belle and Goldman, 1980). In fact, marital status is a major contributing variable to emotional disturbance in women (Gove, 1972 and 1979). Marriage seems to have a "protective" effect on men, but a negative effect on women. Married men have significantly fewer mental health problems, while married women have more problems than *either* single women *or* single men. Marital difficulty is the most commonly reported event in the six months prior to the onset of depression and the most frequent problem presented by depressed women (Paykel et al., 1969). In contrast, a confiding, intimate relationship with a spouse can be an important protection against depression in the face of life stress (Brown and Harris, 1978).

The rate of depression among women is currently on the increase (Weissman and Klerman, 1979; Lester, 1979). This seems incongruent with the age of "we've come a long way, baby" when women seem to have gained more equality. A final aspect of the sociocultural theory focuses on rising expectations and recent social change, suggesting that the increased psychological stresses of modern life have their detrimental effects on women in particular. The discrepancy between women's rising expectations (due to the women's movement, legislation and other social change efforts to improve opportunities for women) and the likelihood or reality of reaching those aspirations, is indeed great. Depression occurs not only when conditions are at their worst, but also when aspirations are positively reinforced by promises and a variety of "social change" thrusts. When reality strikes and the dismal prospect of achieving goals is realized, depression, frustration and powerlessness are the result. Change efforts (producing rising expectations which are actually unattainable) can paradoxically cause a higher preponderance of emotional disturbance in women. As an additional stress, recent social change has produced unclear and diffuse expectations for women (Gove, 1979): while a career is valued, so are traditional behaviors which are often antithetical to a career orientation.

An *integrative theory* has been proposed in recognition of the fact that several different types of factors impact on the mental well-being of women (Weissman and Klerman, 1979). Biological/genetic theories, though undeniably feasible, cannot fully explain sex differences in mental health. A sociocultural component must be posited. This is substantiated by repeated findings of the interaction between sex and marital status in relationship to mental disturbances. Only social and environmental factors can explain why married women are predisposed to mental illness, but married men are "protected" from it. A combined model of external stress, internal psychological change and individual vulnerability may be the best explanation of why women are more prone to depression or other types of mental illness. Whether depression will manifest itself is contingent on the adoption and prompt resolution of stressful life events as well as the psychological disposition of the individual. The integrative theory proposes that women are more sensitive to stressors affecting attachment bonds and that there is an interaction between the characteristics of women (biological and/or sociocultural) and their sensitivity to stressors which disrupt these bonds. Since not all persons react in a maladaptive way (e.g., experience depression), an integrative theory seems especially plausible. While stress may act as the catalyst, other factors, such as physiological changes and problems, internal psychological processes, and environmental factors also seem to carry some weight in determining a woman's predisposition to mental illness.

WOMEN WHO ARE NOT MENTAL HEALTH CLIENTS

The mental health problems of women who are not currently formally seeking mental health services are gaining visibility and beginning to permeate the boundaries of the mental health system. Victims of rape and domestic assault, for example, have been traditionally recognized as in need of health care and protection. Only recently, however, have these women been accepted as viable mental health clients, though they often need a type of psychological intervention not readily available in the mental health system. Other groups of women also recognized as in need of special mental health services include: minority women; women who are poor; women in the correctional system; those obtaining, or who have had, abortions; and women in rural settings. As these groups gain more visibility and make their needs known, the necessity of the mental health system responding to these underserved groups of women will become more and more obvious. Underserved populations not only illustrate a lack of available services, but also reflect societal stereotypes. That is, in disorders that *do* fit the feminine sex role stereotype, such as depression, hysteria and phobias, women show higher rates of service utilization than do men (Russo and VandenBos, 1980). Conversely, behaviors exhibited by women that are not congruent with society's view of women's role, such as al-

coholism or drug abuse, are usually ignored in terms of service provision.

Women are experiencing an increase in stress because of
societal changes that have been occurring. More and more
women are entering the work force whether they choose to
or not. In doing so, women may experience difficulties in ar-
ranging for child care and transportation. If they are single
parents, they must juggle all facets of their financial situation. Add to this the fear, despair and possible lack of
self-confidence when first entering a job, and it is understandable that a woman's experience in starting (and maintaining) a job can culminate in some form of emotional disturbance. The old proverb still prevails: ''a woman's work is
never done.'' Oftentimes, she may return home after work
to yet another set of chores. An eight-to-five job for many
women is simply a fallacy.

For those women who choose a career and/or re-enter the
job market as a personal aim—as opposed to those who are
financially forced to—some of the same problems can occur. Women are continually exposed to discrimination with
its ensuing loss of self-esteem. Hard work and a career long
strived for may not fulfill a woman's expectations. The dis-
covery of limited mobility and autonomy in a job, which she
and not her male peers are subject to, can be particularly
disturbing. She learns that equivalent qualifications are not
the key, but that one's sex determines career success.
Again, self-worth is questioned, powerlessness is experienced, and depression may be the inevitable result. Should
she fight for her rights, become assertive and risk having her
femininity questioned or is feigned complacency the answer? As it currently stands, both routes could provide the
basis for a diagnosis of mental illness.

CONCLUSIONS

This section has outlined the sex differences in mental
health problems between men and women. We have also
presented some of the major theories proposed to account
for these differences and the evidence available to support
them. Finally, we have discussed the stresses faced by

women who are not mental health clients and the need to address problems which can exacerbate into emotional disturbance.

The two articles that follow present each author's own perspective on the nature of sex differences in mental health problems and their causes. Teresa Bernardez expands upon how women's socialization increases the stresses placed upon them while shutting off ways to cope effectively with these stresses. She goes on to discuss how lack of recognition of the impact of female socialization produces inappropriate treatment in the mental health system. Jean Baker Miller presents a sociocultural perspective on women's mental health problems and identifies promising, non-traditional service alternatives to build on women's strengths.

Prevalent Disorders of Women: Attempts Toward a Different Understanding and Treatment

Teresa Bernardez

As a psychiatrist at Michigan State University, Department of Psychiatry, my primary interest since coming to the University in 1971 has been the mental health of women. My own research, teaching, and training primarily concerns women's issues. My point of view needs to be clarified, because I do not see myself among the majority of psychiatrists. This is partially because of my sex, which means I belong to the ten percent of my profession who are women psychiatrists. But also because my own view of what affects women and leads to so-called "mental illness" is very different from the prevailing views in psychiatry—and that should be known. I believe that everybody has personal biases. There are no psychiatrists who don't have them. The public has the right to know what they are. I will be presenting my emphasis on social views of femininity and how they define women's disorders. My views about mental health problems in women are based upon a feminist perspective.

My presentation concerns prevailing disorders of women—those disorders of women that are prevalent in this culture, at this time. It is important to talk about culture because the problems of women vary with the culture and also vary with the times and situations during which the culture is being observed. I also hope to shed new light on old dilemmas that women have had, for instance, depression. Women as well as men have been depressed for centuries.

Presented at the Michigan Department of Mental Health Women's Task Force Public Forum, "An Overview of Women's Mental Health Problems," Lansing, Michigan, September 19, 1980.

Dr. Bernardez is a psychiatrist and full-time faculty in the Department of Psychiatry, Michigan State University. She has been active in national, state and professional activities concerning women's mental health problems and treatment.

17

Depression is not new. But there is a new understanding of this disorder for women which should be compared with traditional understandings to see why the present approaches to the treatment of women need to be examined and substantially altered. I will also address treatment issues and issues of prevention because many want to know what can be done prior to the time when the woman is ill.

FACTORS AFFECTING WOMEN'S MENTAL HEALTH

I would like to concern myself first with the impact of several factors that I think psychiatrists and mental health workers do not pay enough attention to in regard to women. One is the *socialization of women.* Each culture socializes women in particular ways, expecting certain behaviors that are called normal. Those expected behaviors may come to be regarded as natural but they are not. The ideas of femininity that the culture holds acceptable or appropriate for women have enormous influence on what is considered "ill" or deviant behavior.

Second, is the *social status of women.* The reality is that in our society, the social status of women is low. Women have a second class citizenship, and that has implications for their mental health.

The third important factor to keep in mind is *discrimination against women.* Discrimination in employment and in education (two crucial areas for women) is linked to the acquisition of certain mental illnesses because health has to do with the kind of economic power women have, the kind of employment they have, and the kind of education women can potentially acquire.

The fourth important factor is the *biases that support inequality* for women among the public and among mental health workers (since we are no different than the public at large). We have certain prejudices that affect what we believe women should be like and we call that "health." We should be very careful to examine what has been passed as healthy for women, because when we alter our standards of what is healthy, the treatments "of certain diseases of women" are also very different. One of the treatments, for instance, might be to reach equality for women, to increase the right of women to make the same amount of money for the same amount of work. This doesn't seem to have anything to do with mental health, and yet it would eradicate some of the causes of the distress that women present.

Turning to the *socialization of women:* We have discovered that women are socialized in ways that make them particularly likely to develop certain troubles. For instance, the so-called "feminine" characteristics of women are not a biological fact but are acquired through socialization and the interplay of complex forces in the environment. One of those is very prominent in any discussion of depression: the imposed societal prescription that a woman be at the service of others rather than at the service of herself and others. The second is the strong discouragement and punishment of women's aggressiveness. I use aggressiveness as a neutral term indicating any kind of activity directed toward action on behalf of the self as well as the expression of negative affects (from anger to rebellion, criticism, or displeasure). An important part of what has been called being "feminine" has been the denial and prohibition of aggressiveness: if you are "feminine" you do not become angry, you do not contradict your elders or people in power or men. If you go against this prohibition, your sexual identity may be questioned. Now that is a very serious thing to do to a human being. When anybody questions the integrity of our sexual identity—our basic sense of self—people tend to tremble a little. And we live in a world in which there is a massive insistence that women ought to be non-aggressive, not angry, not active in ways that may displease or cause problems in the social world. So, if they are angry, active or unpleasant, they may receive a label on their behavior that is totally inappropriate. Femininity as it has been defined by the culture, has had a very serious impact on the confidence of women because women believe that when they are angry there is something wrong with them. And the point that needs attention is that there are always at least *two* partners in this situation. Whenever a woman is angry, one has to examine the partner (the family, the husband, the social milieu) before making any judgments. I have seen enormous damage done to women because of the emphasis placed on responsibility for pathology that they did not in fact have, when the origin of the problem was really in the social world around them.

If a woman is in distress and she has the privileges that the culture decides are enough for her, she may tend to assume that the distress is her fault, that there is something wrong with her. One metaphor I use frequently is that when one has a pain in one's foot, one has to look at the size of the shoe one may be wearing. There may be nothing wrong with the foot itself, if the trouble is that the shoe is a size too small for it. In fact, after wearing shoes that are too small, not only will you have a pain in your foot (so something would be wrong with your foot), but also your foot may become deformed, inclining you to believe that it is a problem of the foot alone. It is much easier to see the metaphor: foot–shoe than to see the metaphor: woman–family–society. But that is what we have to constantly keep in mind.

The social status of women: Everyone is aware of the struggle for equality. It is clear that we are far from making it: that women are not in positions of hierarchy and decision making or in educational circles enough to make a difference; discrimination continues to keep women from gaining access to academic posts in universities and other positions of influence. The rampant and pervasive *discrimination against women* (the third factor) and their subordinate status has a definite impact on mental health (Carmen, Russo and Miller, 1981). Women see themselves as responsible for their social status as second class citizens, which lowers their self-esteem and compounds their problems further by preventing them from utilizing their talents. Therefore, many women are kept from knowing what they are capable of accomplishing. The fourth factor, *biases supporting inequality,* is very profound and very serious. These biases are extremely important in any attempt to deal with the mental health of women. The biases are shared by women themselves. But to make it worse, the people who treat women are also members of the society and they hold the same kind of assumptions about what women's goals should be, which our patients tend to adopt (Broverman, Broverman and Clarkson, 1970).

PREVALENT DISORDERS OF WOMEN

Presently, the most common are: depression, agoraphobia (the fear of open spaces, the fear of moving away from home), psychosomatic disorders in the genital/reproductive tract, marital and family problems. Bulimia is another disorder found prominently among women, particularly young women. Eating disorders in general will be found among women in great numbers. Of all these common disorders, depression is the most prevalent.

Recent studies have emphasized how social factors contribute to the gender difference. They contend that depression affects females mostly because females have been reared and socialized in order to accept what is called "learned helplessness." Taboos on anger and aggressive behavior compound the trouble (Bernardez, 1978). Aggressive and angry behavior are defined by the culture as hurtful, offensive or destructive acts when women enact them. Those prohibitions act against a woman being assertive, supporting herself, speaking with authority, complaining directly and explicitly, moving energetically to carry out a function, directing, or organizing. All of these functions are constructive and helpful to the self but require aggressive energy so women cannot freely exercise them because of the ways femininity is defined.

If the female is a second class citizen, discriminated against, with not much chance to exercise power and/or change her environment, and she cannot even be angry because that doesn't fit her sex role, depression is a very natural outcome. You don't need to be a mental health professional to understand that if these are the conditions in which you live, and you cannot protest against them because when you do you are told that that is not "feminine" behavior and your sexual identity is questioned, you are going to be depressed.

If you accept the cultural prescriptions, you may complain in self-defeating ways because of these prohibitions. The energetic and self-assertive protest that may be required and the demand that others change when that demand is appropriate, is impossible if you have internalized such prescribed ways of being "feminine." Focusing your grievances and addressing them seriously requires that you disregard acceptable feminine behavior. The role of psychosocial factors in depression clarify why women are depressed more often than men.

Another important determinant of depression in women is their role in families. Statistically, the mental health of married women is lower than single women's and married men's mental health (Bernard, 1972). In fact, men profit from being married, from a mental health point of view; for women the reverse is true. And while single men suffer more often from psychological ailments, single women are in better health. These are interesting facts. How are we to interpret these findings? My interpretation, confirmed by my clinical experience with couples and families is that women's married role generates stress. Women are very much responsible for the health of the whole family. They are "other" directed, they are told that they should *do* for others. And they *are* more empathic than men. They are also the persons primarily responsible for the rearing of children. They tend to be responsible for the emotional life and health of the whole family to their own detriment, because nobody does that for them. Men are not socialized to do that for women, and they certainly do not rear children. So women do not have much help. I believe that the responsibilities for care and empathy of others plus the unavailability of support and empathy for them has a negative effect. We need to establish that men should be socialized to be empathic too so that the job does not fall only on the shoulders of women.

Beavers (1977) is a good example of how blind an otherwise sensitive observer and researcher of families can be. In his Timberlane family studies, he distinguishes between average, healthy and optimally functioning families. Both average and healthy families function well. There is no contradiction, however, when he finds that they function well but the wives are depressed. He still calls that a healthy family. The crucial member for the emotional well-being of that family is not well and yet he calls that a "healthy family." That is very telling: how even sensitive people are completely unaware that "healthy families" function well at the expense of women. The female is able to produce a "healthy family"; meaning everybody but her is in good shape. The conclusion appears inevitable that the female's social function is to produce a healthy family even, if in the process, she herself becomes depressed. This example underlines the importance of examining what is considered "healthy" and what is the behavior and experience of women when talking about ideal or positive family outcomes. It is important to know who defines that outcome. Is it a good outcome for a woman to be a submissive creature who doesn't complain, who appears depressed but has a "healthy family?" Who should insist that a positive outcome in family studies must include the woman herself: that she displays some characteristics that we consider healthy for everybody, not just for men. Positive outcome would no longer be a matter of absence of depression or symptoms, but rather how creative, how able, how autonomous, how personally competent, how in control of her life the woman in question is? It would not be any different for men. It follows that when evaluating treatment outcomes for women, we need to recognize that we have pervasive biases telling us that a woman who is healthy is a woman who: keeps her mouth shut, demands nothing, and has learned to adapt to it.

Psychoanalytic psychotherapies, for instance, have been criticized for emphasizing the intrapsychic nature of patients' problems rather than accounting for their origins within the social milieu. The woman is thus made responsible for her troubles through a diagnosed deficiency when her ailment is really a symptom of her adaptation to a world that has pathogenic expectations about her. This is a true and serious criticism of psychoanalysis and other psychotherapies. Most systems of psychotherapy do not examine the role of socialization in women. Most individual psychotherapists are ignorant of systems theory. You cannot, in this day and age, examine a woman without examining what is happening in the system where she moves: what is happening in her family, what kind of stresses she is trying to overcome, what her financial and educational situation is. Psychotherapies which do not closely examine the role of culture and the social context in which the woman lives obscure the problem, misdiagnose it, and mistreat the woman patient.

A serious criticism can also be aimed at psychopharmacological therapies. At present, all psychopharmacological treatments aim at the alleviation of symptoms. There are no drugs that "cure" any mental disorder. The crucial question to ask is "when and why are drugs prescribed for women?" Minor tranquilizers are often prescribed erroneously for undiagnosed depression. All tranquilizers shut off the signals of distress, decrease the irritation and the anxiety, in every case. But if we regard a woman's condition as generally producing stress, to diminish the symptom does nothing to eradicate the cause. In fact, pharmacological treatment may tend to confirm the woman's impression that something is wrong with her, may diminish the "nuisance value" of the symptom, obscure a solution to the underlying problem, and promote a passive stance in women. Psychopharmacological treatment can be a useful adjunct to other therapeutic efforts designed to correct the underlying problem. But medication alone has been used frequently to silence the distress of women and to diminish the conscious pain they are suffering. If you believe that anxiety and depression are signs of a problem that needs to be addressed, a diminution of such "symptoms" is not only *not helpful* but perhaps *harmful.* If you believe that the "problem" may not be that of the woman in question, the use of medication can no longer be called "treatment."

It is, therefore, very important in the case of women and medications to ask who we are treating and for what. In actual practice, the woman may be silenced from rightful complaints about her husband or job or family which others prefer not to hear. A similar danger may occur with hospitalizations. Let me cite an example. In entering the admissions ward of a hospital, I saw a woman with a black eye and I inquired why she was there. The response of the hospital staff was "she is hysterical." The term "hysterical" used for women means out of control. When men are out of control they are never called hysterical. It is a pejorative term for women. Loss of control is very unpalatable, unladylike. When I inquired more about the history, I heard this woman had been beaten by her husband. She had been crying and she was frightened. *She* was hospitalized with a diagnosis of hysteria; *her husband* stayed at home. There was no malevolent intent in the hospitalization. Those involved wanted to preserve her security, and to offer a refuge. But nonetheless *she* becomes a patient with a diagnostic label—not the person who assaulted her. With all good intention, the victim is further victimized. It is fundamental to look at the woman's environment in order not to misinterpret and misjudge. When women are hospitalized, *look* at where they are coming from: look not only at the woman herself and her reactions because if you look only at this "hysterical" woman, you may in fact agree that she shows loss of impulse control and "labile affect" or other signs of a disturbance. Look at her *whole* situation, at the social context and the conditions in which she lives. She may have been labeled as a psychiatric patient for a trouble none of her making.

SELECTION OF TREATMENT APPROACHES

We have data indicating that women learn much better about the impact of social factors impinging on their behavior in groups than in individual contacts. Groups, however, are not a favored modality in agencies. It takes a great deal more skill to treat patients successfully in groups. In our own state, mental health workers have difficulty getting training in group psychotherapy. Michigan State University is the only training site that has a group skills training program and because of funding cuts, it has been reduced to one year. Many mental health professionals continue to be trained exclusively in the practice of individual therapy and, therefore, practice individual therapy. If you don't know how to treat people in a group, you are not likely to choose a group modality. It follows that although women are more likely to discover the common denominators of feminine distress in a group of women, they are likely to be offered individual counseling. This doesn't mean that I am in favor of group therapy for every woman or that women should never have individual therapy. My point is that the skills required to treat many women helpfully and economically are not available and that the training for those skills is scarce. If you are going to have therapists in a women's group, make sure they are women. A group of women led by a male reproduces the situation of subordination in the social world and prevents the all-female composition that is so fruitful in addressing and resolving women's concerns (Bernardez, 1983).

Women could form groups of their own making. It would be even more efficient to encourage women to decide on the group composition themselves and offer only the skills that would be specifically required. This may counter the dependent position which many women assume when they ask for help. Leaderless groups have been particularly helpful. The research on the effects of consciousness raising groups alerts us to the potential efficacy of this approach in therapy for women. Another issue in dealing with the problems of women is to replace traditional treatments with the development of skills to better cope with the environment. Assertiveness training, for instance, has been very helpful to women when done by informed and experienced therapists. It is economical, efficient, and a very appropriate strategy for interpersonal change.

TRAINING MENTAL HEALTH PROFESSIONALS AND GENDER ROLE AWARENESS

Mental health professionals should be required to know a lot more than they now do about non-traditional treatment approaches for women, research data on sex role socialization and the effects of discrimination on mental health. For instance, the effects of gender are lost on many therapists who continue to believe it does not matter.

A male therapist has to be especially knowledgeable about the role he automatically plays in the treatment of any woman for being a man and an authority. If he is not aware of it, he is likely to be an inadequate therapist. Women therapists do not have to worry about this because women are not assumed to be the authority and the power that rules the world. Research studies show that male therapists tend to expect more traditional behaviors than female therapists, in both men and women. Men tend to prefer female patients, for obvious reasons. Female patients are for the most part more empathic, more aware of their troubles, more verbal, more capable of expressing themselves, more motivated for treatment than men.

They are also more submissive, more passive, more admiring, less questioning. Therefore, when male therapists treat female patients, the important variable is how tolerant and well informed is that man. How tolerant is he of the capacity of that female to question his judgment, to make a decision that is not agreed to by him? And how does he feel in that type of situation. Males are socialized in our culture to assume "naturally" a position of authority and to react negatively to assertive or aggressive behavior in the female. Although mental health workers presumably should be less biased and more tolerant than the rest of the population, studies show that this is not the case when it comes to aggressive behavior in females (aggressive meaning taking initiative, being self-assured, or questioning the sagacity of the therapist). So here we need to have the therapist well aware and informed. And if you want to increase awareness of the biases on mental health professionals, you have to do it in groups too. Awareness of sex role bias does not come through didactic seminars. You cannot teach people what they are blind to; you have to show them through experience. We have found that for both sexes, the most effective way is to place psychotherapists in a group with others to examine their own sex role behavior and assumptions, and to see how these affect their judgment in relation to men and women. Only then could we really presume that reading the available literature or lectures would have any effect on them.

We also need to pay attention to the supervision of mental health professionals. The issue of cross-sex supervision is quite important. It has been demonstrated that females are more likely to empathize with males than the reverse. It is important to emphasize that when a person of the opposite sex is treating a patient—in cross-sex therapy—the supervisor should be the same sex as the patient, if possible. Female supervisors could in this way introduce awareness of bias in the male therapist and help clarify the misjudgments and wrong assumptions common in the treatment of women.

Many men can identify with females only partially; their own socialization prohibits their complete identification with women. They cannot show empathy for some aspects of the female because they have vested interests (conscious or unconscious) in maintaining their own positions of power. So unless they have excellent professional training and they have lives that most men in this culture have not been able to have, they fail to understand what women with less training know only too well. This issue is of importance because at this moment, if women were more assertive, and more free to be critical of doctors, they could be relied upon to change the situation that pervades the health care system. But the problem is that we are in the midst of a situation in which women are continuously reinforced in behaviors that help them to be victimized. And since there are few women training physicians and still too few women medical doctors, physicians are unlikely to deal with women in different ways.

INSTITUTIONAL AND SOCIAL CHANGE

To change views and behavior about the treatment of women, you have to affect the people who make the decisions at the higher levels. But how many women are in administrative positions; how many women are superintendents of hospitals; how many women are clinical directors; how many women decide what a milieu program in a hospital will be like; how many women make any decisions about budgeting in the mental health department? It is logical to assume that until we have more women in these positions, the treatment of women will suffer. The lesser paid mental health workers are women. Those powerless in terms of decision making are women. There are some things that cannot be heard and implemented unless women are in positions of authority, direct programs and manage budgets. One cannot be accomplished without the other. At Michigan State University, we have a psychiatry department with some 50 faculty members. Of those faculty members, 18 are tenured members; of those 18 tenured faculty, only one (me) is a woman. In the positions where greater power can be exercised, we see less and less women. And you know that that makes a difference; a psychiatrist is more powerful, a tenured faculty member can take risks. There is no way in which men in power can have that sense of empathy that comes from having shared a disadvantaged status. And it is delusional to count on the good graces of men. Men stand to lose their privileges if women assume equality. They should be glad to lose them because the price they pay for them is enormous. But until men are aware of this price, we can expect very slow progress in this area. It is thus essential that more women move up in the world.

Women's Mental Health Issues: Moving Forward With Awareness and Program Alternatives

Jean Baker Miller

THEORETICAL HISTORY AND ITS EFFECTS

In the last decade, virtually all of the received wisdom about the mental health of women has been questioned, and in many instances overturned. We now have a body of more valid data (Carmen et al., 1981, and several others) and the beginnings of new theory (Miller, 1976; Gilligan, 1982; Jorden et al., 1982). However, much remains to be done.

Until about ten years ago, the underlying theory, clearly reflecting the cultural view of women, said, in essence, that the psychology of women followed from the famous psychoanalytic triad, that is, that women were inherently passive, narcissistic and masochistic. The aim of women's psychological development was to reach the correct reconciliation to this inherent "truth." Any tendencies which deviated from this aim were, by definition, pathological.

While this statement may sound startling today, just a short time ago it was extraordinarily difficult to suggest anything different within professional circles. Pausing for a moment to note this contrast may give us encouragement.

The prevalent theory would not have been so important if its effects had been limited to a small wealthy group. However, the theory formed the basis for education and practice in a wide range of disciplines such as social work, education, nursing, counseling, psychology and psychiatry. It also permeated media that was directed to an even wider public, for example, through books about raising

Based on a paper previously published in the *Journal of the American Medical Women's Association,* reprinted with permission.

Dr. Miller is a psychiatrist and Director of The Stone Center for Developmental Services and Studies, Wellesley College, Massachusetts.

children. Most importantly, it affected people who would never be able to pay a psychiatrist, but who, because of poverty and/or powerlessness, are often affected by public institutions such as social agencies, welfare departments, schools, clinics and hospitals.

Most of the recent "revolution" in theory and knowledge has not yet been incorporated into the training of professionals. Thus, we can identify immediately one huge need. One implication of this gap is that professionals still start out with a handicap, i.e., an erroneous socialization into a profession which is internalized in a thorough-going way. Until this need is addressed, the professional has the necessity to undertake an intellectual and personal reevaluation and undoing of what he or she has already incorporated as "knowledge" and as a set of attitudes and values.

BASIC FACTORS AFFECTING MENTAL HEALTH

In the past, women were defined solely in terms of the family. Society supposedly provided for the woman as the wife and mother. Leaving aside questions about that definition of women, the important current news is that that family structure has already changed. If the traditional structure was defined as an employed husband, a wife not employed outside the home and having the major responsibility for care of family and home and one or more dependent children, only seven to sixteen percent of the population fit this picture. The exact percentages vary with different authors. The major reason for this small percentage is the second notable new feature, that is, the high percentage of women who are working. Women's contribution to the economy raised many two-parent families somewhat above the poverty line; it is said to have been the margin that kept the total economy going by virtue of enabling families to purchase major commodities such as electrical appliances and the like. And for some families, mainly single-parent families, the woman is the sole earner (Carmen et al., 1981).

What has not changed is *where* women work. For 80% of women, it is still in the lowest paid, most dead-end segment of the labor force—and the work place site most productive of stress (Carmen et al., 1981).

It's important to note, however, that according to several recent national surveys, there have been significant changes in the last 15 years in women's attitudes about their "proper place" and their own needs (Veroff et al., 1981; Parents Magazine Survey, 1982).

Economists tell us that we face the prospect of continuing high unemployment, decreased expenditures on public services, and possibly a combination of these with inflation. The major societal factors will lead to increased stress for many people, but more stress for those who suffer even in times of affluence, i.e., the poor, minorities, the elderly, and women. Women, of course, make up a disproportionate majority of the people in the other major poverty categories. Thus, we look to the "feminization of poverty," meaning that except for a very small percentage of others, the poor will be women and their dependent children (Carmen et al., 1981).

What have we learned, then, from new psychological theory and knowledge that might guide us in the face of these conditions? We have learned that helplessness has a devastating effect on health and mental health. This means that despite the particulars of any individual's life history (and these are of course important), when a person feels on many fronts—economic, social, political and psychological—that he or she does not have some possibility of exerting effective action—of having an impact on his or her immediate life conditions and relationships—the psychological balance shifts to an inability to use and to build on—or even to recognize the existence of—his or her psychological resources. All mental health work, *perforce,* rests on the ability to elucidate and build on the person's existing or potential psychological resources. (It is important to note that the impact women desire and the way women may validly prefer to act is very different from the way these things have been defined to date, but that is another very large topic in itself; e.g., Miller, 1976; Gilligan, 1982; Jordan, Surrey, Kaplan, 1982; Miller 1982; Stiver, 1982).

In the overall, it's probably fairly accurate to predict that members of each sex will react to such circumstances differently. Women may fall into certain tendencies following from the cultural forces which still affect us. The dangers will be an increase in women's fear of effective words and actions; lack of assertion of needs and rights or more extremely, loss of all recognition that each one of us has needs; and, most basically, loss of the sense that we have the right to have them—and to define them, to say what we believe they are.

Second, women often still have a tendency toward exaggerated feelings of inadequacy and self-blame, often when this is clearly in contradiction to their *demonstrated* effectiveness and worth. That is, we women still tend internally to blame ourselves more readily for all that goes wrong, not only in our own lives, but in the lives of those in relation to us; for example, children, husbands, parents, friends and others. I would emphasize how common these tendencies still are in many women, even in many women who are *doing* very important things. But this may not be so surprising when we recall how strong the cultural traditions producing these tendencies have been. Moreover, the world in general still stands ready to reinforce these parts of ourselves.

For men, we might predict that the broad societal forces, such as unemployment, can lead to feelings which may be very similar at bottom, like helplessness and inability to act effectively. (A difference here is that this point is compounded for women precisely because women have been told that a situation of helplessness and powerlessness was "normal," "women's rightful place," "part of women's identity," and the like.) Despite the evidence that men, too, may have an underlying tendency to feel inadequate in the face of bad external conditions, evidence suggests that men are more likely to make these tendencies manifest in destructive or nonproductive action directed outward against others. That is to say, in addition to alcoholism and drug addiction, there is the beating of wives, rape on the street, sexual harassment in the work place—and possibly more angry backlash against women on all levels—economic, political and personal (and possibly against other powerless groups such as minority groups and children). This, then, is to predict continued attacks on those still less powerful than unemployed or financially stressed white men.

PROGRAMS

What can mental health professionals and allied groups do? Shall we advocate that women and other less powerful groups give up their struggle for full personhood and participation?

Quite the contrary. I believe the recent knowledge allows us to sketch a program for action. Undoubtedly there are many ways to formulate a program, but I'd suggest the following as first priorities. First, we can continue to point to major societal forces rather than starting at the wrong end by blaming the victims. In so doing, we can heavily emphasize prevention. Next, we can support the voice and the actions of women consumers. Women are the *key* consumers in the health and mental health systems at this time.

Prevention

We now have data to suggest probable priorities for prevention.

1. We know that *appropriate* help is still needed by practically all women at certain life phases, and that it can have a strong preventive effect. These phases actually begin at birth, or before. Women have developed effective programs for pregnancy, birth and the post-partum period (for example, the post-partum program in Vancouver described by Robertson, 1980). Strengthening women's psychological resources could occur through specific attention to girls in nursery school, primary school, and especially at adolescence. The stages of marriage and young motherhood are ones requiring particular attention (see the discussion of depression below). Definite help can be given at the famous midlife period, and also to meet the particular needs of older women.

We now know that the kind of help given in the past at each of these life phases would have been wrong. As an example of "overturning" old formulations, Rubin (1979) brings evidence to suggest that the key concern for women in midlife is not really the "empty nest," nor the old "menopausal depression," but the issue of a continuing struggle to define a sense of self and to put it into action in the world.

2. In addition to the help that all women need, there are traumas that assault many women. Preventive action should be increased to stop these. Until they are stopped, the programs women have developed can reduce the serious long-term effects. This means help for victims of incest and other childhood sexual assaults, rape victims, battered women and for women suffering all forms of victimization.

3. We can build on the good studies which now allow us to pinpoint other specific actions. Prevention of depression can be used as an example to suggest interventions in several other areas such as phobias, alcoholism, substance abuse, etc.

Depression is one of the most common mental health problems. It is twice as common in women as in men (Weissman and Klerman, 1977). The highest rates are not, as usually believed, "menopausal women," but in women in the young adult age group, the age at which those women who are mothers are most involved in the raising of young children. Here depression does not occur in all women equally, but has been found to be five times more frequent in working class mothers than in middle class mothers (Brown and Harris, 1978). Thus, depression has far-reaching effects on women and when women are mothers, there are also serious effects on their children (Belle, 1982).

Here is a clear area for preventive work. Specific guidelines are suggested by the findings of several recent studies (Belle, 1982; Brown and Harris, 1978). The major relevant factors are: (a) conditions of high stress and demand; (b) reduced ability to act effectively on the immediate conditions of one's life; (c) lack of validation, affirmation and support for one's felt experience by the significant people in one's life. There is also evidence of other specific factors, e.g., lack of employment outside the home correlates with a higher rate of depression, even in young mothers (Brown and Harris, 1978). This finding suggests that while there is still much stress in combining both home and outside work, it may be worse *not* to be working.

4. There is another topic that we must face as professionals. An area of major risk for women has been encounters with the health or mental health professions. Many women have now documented this in various ways (Belle, 1982; Cooperstock, 1976). One of the many examples was the overprescription of tranquilizers for women (Cooperstock, 1976).

Consumers

In the past decade, women have accomplished not only a phenomenal critique, but, in many instances, the creation of new alternatives in the health and mental health fields. With very little money and against great odds, women, themselves, have provided help to each other in ways that build strength and self-esteem, rather than increase feelings of inadequacy and/or dependency on those who are cast in the mold of superiors, authorities or "experts." (Remember, these were the experts who had a theory about what women were and what women needed.) Examples of these phenomenal accomplishments are such programs as rape crisis centers, shelters for battered women, post-partum help, childbirth programs, and many others.

Out of this experience, these groups of women now have a vast body of extremely valuable knowledge and know-how. Professionals have not yet learned and benefited from this body of knowledge about women, and about how to help women to help themselves best.

WOMEN AS A NEW FORCE

A true alliance of women consumers and women mental health workers could constitute a new force in the mental health system. Moreover, other trends are in motion to augment this potential. Women are one-third of the students at many medical schools and more in other disciplines. If this large group of new professionals were able to unite with the body of women consumers who have mobilized to assert their health and mental health needs, would we not be able to have a major effect? Could we not change the face of health and mental health institutions?

These numbers of women represent a potential for *real* power. What may hold us back is—and it will be characteristic of many powerless groups, but perhaps especially of women—lack of recognition and consciousness that we are in a position to wield such power.

For professionals, I believe the first step is to look at this possibility and then to examine honestly and self-critically, but also optimistically, those factors which may be impeding professional women from seeing how we can change things for the better *for ourselves* within the professions by joining with women who have not been socialized into the professions. We must examine the forces still within us which keep us from using ourselves fully and freely as women and from joining with other women in this struggle for the hopes and visions that I believe many of us share.

SECTION 2:
SEXIST TREATMENT IN THE
MENTAL HEALTH SYSTEM:
THE EVIDENCE

Recognizing the important differences between women's and men's mental health problems is a recent development. This recognition has been aided greatly by the women's movement, although for some time the literature has clearly established higher rates for women of depression, certain types of phobias, and eating disorders. We also know that high levels of stress, particularly continued over time, correlate strongly with depression and that women *continue* to be the majority consumers of the mental health delivery system in a variety of service settings and modalities. Issues common to women have emerged across numerous individual cases, demonstrating that women's mental health problems must be seen within a larger societal context. What is happening to women that is making them more vulnerable to certain types of disorders? What is the mental health delivery system doing (or not doing) for women once they become clients? Is current treatment by the mental health system helping them, or is it perhaps exacerbating their problems? The President's Commission on Mental Health (1978) felt that traditionally trained mental health professionals are not adequately prepared to deal with the problems of contemporary women or to help women confront difficulties caused by ''powerlessness, alienation and frustration.'' Russo and Hilberman (1979) succinctly summarize the issues involved:

37

Poverty, alienation, and powerlessness all characterize women's status, to the detriment of their mental health. The psychological consequences of women's disadvantaged status are severe, hidden and a great cost of our society. Such problems as alcoholism; drug abuse; depression; rape; domestic violence; incest and unwanted pregnancy are all inadequately or inappropriately addressed, and all are reflective of women's inability to control the outcome of their daily lives. The mental health professionals have been part of the problem. Rather than addressing causes, mental health professionals have attended to the symptoms of women's second class status. While treatment of symptoms is a legitimate professional effort, there is an increasing recognition of the ethical obligation to go further. (p. 2)

The mental health delivery system needs to examine whether it is sensitive enough to the norms of women's lives and the effects of their pervasive powerlessness and second class status. Women's mental health issues that revolve around role and role overload can no longer be ignored.

This section is concerned with the broad aspects of what happens to women once they become clients of the system. Do women experience sex bias from clinicians? Are there sex differences in medication practices? What do we know about some of the more non-traditional treatment modalities being used for women? These are some of the questions and issues that will be, and need to be addressed.

SEX BIASES OF CLINICIANS

The problem of bias in the therapeutic relationship has always been an important one because of the potentially powerful and influential role of the therapist. Since discriminatory practices and sex biases are part of the attitudes and stereotypes common in our society today and a majority of the clients in the mental health system are women while a majority of psychologists and psychiatrists are men, the examination of sexual biases is critical. Surface biases are apparent in mental health services: few programs specific to the female experience exist. Of critical interest is whether a woman's therapist may be an ineffective helper because of his or her biases, or even worse, may exacerbate the very problem a female client seeks to resolve. The existence of such biases was the focus of a study by Broverman et al. (1970) which concluded that clinical judgments about healthy female traits and healthy male traits differ.

Broverman et al. hypothesized that clinical judgments of the characteristics of healthy individuals would differ according to the sex of the person judged and that those differences would parallel stereotypic sex role differences. They also hypothesized that criteria considered healthy for an adult (sex unspecified) would most resemble those behaviors considered healthy for men, not women. Both of these hypotheses were confirmed. In effect, this confirmation of sex-specific norms of mental health clearly shows that a double standard of mental health exists for men and women. This places women in a conflict. If they exhibit behavior that is considered "healthy" for men and adults, they are behaving in a manner inappropriate to their sex role. However, if they behave in a manner appropriate to their sex role, they must accept its concomitant second class and unhealthy status. This is a clear example of the double bind in which women find themselves.

In a similar study (Fabricant, 1974), therapists rated negatively 68-70% of adjectives they assigned to the female role and rated positively 67-71% of the words assigned to the male role. In fact, most studies on the subject show evidence of stereotyping and many show that male clinicians stereotype more than females, although these attitudes *do* appear to liberalize over time (Brodsky and Hare-Mustin, 1980). However, no study has been done to relate sexist bias in therapy to client outcome. Some critics contend that, although double *standards* may exist, scientifically acceptable evidence is still insufficient to establish that sexism is widespread in psychotherapy (Maffeo, 1979).

Recent studies on language interactions between men and women can shed light on the sex bias question, since therapy is basically a verbal relationship, usually involving a male therapist and a female client. In conversations, males make 98% of the interruptions; women try more often than men to begin a conversation while succeeding far less often (Thorne, 1980). This suggests that male-dominated inter- actions may often occur in mixed-sex verbal interactions in- cluding therapy. A devaluation of the woman in the treat- ment setting would be the inescapable conclusion. How can a woman expect to be taken seriously when she is inter- rupted or not really listened to at all? The failure of men to understand female experience and to take it seriously has been often asserted. This failure, combined with stereo- typed biases, played out through inappropriate language in- teractions and more subtle, non-verbal methods of influenc- ing clients' behaviors (Franks, 1979) could harm, more than help, female clients.

Given that therapist sex biases exist and assuming that these affect the mental health treatment provided, there are many problematic implications for women as mental health clients. First, and foremost, is the fostering of traditional roles and behavior at the expense of individual female integ- rity. ''Mentally healthy'' attributes of women are defined as the traditionally feminine ones—passivity, emotionality, de- pendency, etc. If a woman deviates from this role, her men- tal health may be questioned. When soliciting professional help to overcome burdens in striving to become indepen- dent, for example, a woman may instead be advised to abandon that aim. Thus, in attempting to obtain help in achieving her goal of independence, the woman not only does not receive that help, but is encouraged to fulfill the traditional female role. The therapist's insensitivity to a woman's concerns and aims can only compound her anxi- ety and mental instability. Emotional help sought by women (which may or may not be given at all) may be contingent, not on a woman's individual aspirations, but to what extent she adheres to societal norms and role expectations.

Diagnosis, as well as treatment may be based on stereo- typical assumptions. Women may be diagnosed as mentally ill for exhibiting certain traits that in men are considered healthy, such as expressing anger. Male expression of anger, verbally or physically, is viewed as normal behavior. For women, societal role expectations dictate that anger should not be felt, must less expressed. So when a woman openly and blatantly shows her anger, for whatever reason, she may be perceived as having mental problems. Even if the anger is justified—she's lost a loved one, her job, or her self-pride—a woman is supposed to maintain composure and accept loss as a part of life. Because of sex bias, a treatment of female clients may be inappropriate as well as ineffective.

A Task Force on Sex Bias and Sex Role Stereotyping (appointed by the American Psychological Association) identified problems in treatment resulting from therapists' lack of knowledge of women's issues and female development and lack of awareness of their own values and how they may be imposing them on female patients, e.g:

> The female patient. . .may be struggling with her fear of success. . .yet the therapist may be totally unaware of the conflict. Seduction by her father may be overlooked because the therapist is fixated on Freud's Oedipal theory of the child as the source of the sexual impulse. (APA Task Force Report, 1975, p. 1169)

Franks (1979) concluded that for most therapists, ignorance of their own attitude toward sex-role identification "is the rule rather than the exception at the present time" (p. 455).

If the clinician is not in touch with the effects of sexism in his or her own developmental history, then problems in treatment and determination of successful outcomes may arise.

One study reported that according to many women who have been in treatment, the community mental health system is "primarily engaged in adjusting women to existing societal reality" (Women's Task Force Position Paper, 1980, p. 13). The Michigan's Women's Task Force was given some specific examples of this: women who reported feeling unhappy and unfulfilled in their marriages were advised to "go back home"; a couple, now divorced, was advised in therapy that the wife should "stay home more and give more time to her husband," although this had never been presented to the therapist as a problem, nor did the husband perceive it to be one; threatened by expressions of

anger during therapy, women are advised to be ''more feminine'' or are given psychotropic medication. Perhaps the
most common example of sex bias in therapy is mothers being explicitly or implicitly blamed for their children's emotional or adjustment problems. The term ''schizophrenogen-
ic'' (schizophrenia-causing) mother may be out of vogue,
but the concept is not. Children brought into mental health
clinics may be seen alone; their mothers may also be seen
alone as clients. Not often enough does the agency *insist*
that mother, child, *and* father be seen together in family
therapy.

The American Psychological Association Task Force
(1975) advised that certain preventative guidelines can be
set up for therapists: (1) not to encourage assumption of
traditional sex roles at the expense of individual integrity;
(2) to be aware of their tendency to devalue women and to
have low expectations for their success; (3) to avoid use of
psychoanalytic concepts in a sexist way; and (4) for male
therapists to be aware of a tendency to view women as sex
objects.

Thus, there definitely are problematic implications and
possibilities for the double standard/double bind affecting
women in therapy. However, there is also no question that
additional research is needed on how sex biases may
operate, how their negative effects can be avoided and how
clinicians can be given knowledge of female development
and made aware of their own values and the implications of
this for therapeutic relationships.

SEXUAL EXPLOITATION

While the existence of sex biases and their potentially
harmful effects on therapy may be debated, there is no
question of the devastating effects of sexual exploitation of
female clients by male therapists. This may occur in a variety of blatant and subtle forms: blatantly through treatment
as sex objects, sexual harassment, or coercion to engage in
sexual relations; or subtly through extended, prolonged
treatment not clinically justified, but designed to benefit the
therapist. To the female client who may find herself ridden

with emotional anxiety, extended treatment may well cause her to question her "recovery" and ultimately her self-worth. This type of treatment is inappropriate and unethical. A female client seeking emotional help and support who finds herself viewed in a purely sexual way will, no doubt, experience further stress. The inherent degradation felt from sexual harassment is exacerbated by society's practice to "blame the victim." She is caught in a no-win situation: a choice between maintaining the treatment relationship, with its sexual overtures in the hope of achieving some emotional stability, or breaking the relationship to risk receiving no mental health treatment at all and possibly blame from others. Sexual harassment can exploit the stereotypic feminine qualities of the woman client through the dominant power of the therapist (APA Task Force, 1975).

Currently, it is not clearly known the extent to which erotic contact between therapists and clients exists. Surveys of therapists and/or clients indicate a small percentage reporting erotic contact; these reports are almost exclusively of male therapists and female clients (Feldon, 1978). Individual studies of physicians and psychologists (Holroyd and Brodsky, 1977; Kardener et al., 1973) find 5-10% reporting having engaged in intercourse with clients; including other erotic contacts, the percentage rises to 19% of male therapists who have been involved sexually. Individual case reports are numerous and continue to appear. Chesler (1973) found 16 out of 60 female psychiatric patients interviewed who reported having sexual relations with or sexual propositions from therapists. Of the cases reported by Dahlberg (1970), most were male therapists over 40, involved with females ten to 25 years younger. More sophisticated research is needed to determine the *extent* of this problem.

While prevalence is still debatable, reviews of individual cases provide a definite statement as to the *results* of sexual involvement with therapists (APA Task Force, 1975). Clients report guilt and shame over their own actions and in enticing the therapist to "cheat"; grief over the loss of the therapeutic relationship; anger and rage due to the loss or their exploitation, or because of what they have to go through to report the therapist's behavior; fear of rejection by loved ones or of harassment if they come forward; depression and loss of self-esteem; ambivalence and confusion; and massive distrust. Many of these feelings persist for years afterward. Clients who are approached but turn down their therapists can also suffer through feelings of guilt, having their refusal interpreted as hostility, or a fear of getting close. More severe effects have also been identified related to client-therapist sexual involvement such as divorce and contemplation of or attempts at suicide (Sundstrom, 1977). Whatever the effect, sexual contact cannot be condoned: the therapist is inappropriately using his enormous power over the client and he is not doing his job.

CONCLUSIONS

Sex bias and sex stereotyping have been documented among mental health therapists. We have described how this may interfere with effective treatment for women or even harm them directly. We have also reviewed the evidence concerning a much more serious form of sexist treatment, sexual exploitation. Whether overt or subtle in nature, sexual exploitation *hurts* clients and *cannot* be condoned. The following articles present the individual experience of researchers, service providers and consumers on how women are treated by their therapists and by the mental health system. These perspectives add to the evidence in presenting a scathing critique of the mental health treatment of women and mandate immediate change.

A Social Perspective on Women's Mental Health Problems

Barrie Thorne

As a researcher and teacher of social psychology, sociology, and women's studies, I have found that recent feminist scholarship provides important insight into women's mental health. My own work centers on the nature of sexual inequality, gender differentiation of language and speech, and the experiences of girls and women in families, workplaces, and schools.

Within the last decade, the women's movement has helped bring about important breakthroughs—even a revolution—in consciousness and knowledge. We have discovered that much of received knowledge which has been generalized as "human" in fact is based on men's experiences. Women's lives, history, and experiences have either been invisible and erased, or, where present, distorted and devalued. Women's voices are beginning to emerge, challenging and reconstructing traditional knowledge in psychology, sociology, history, literature, biology, and other fields.

For example, by taking women's experiences seriously, Carol Gilligan (1982) transformed Lawrence Kohlberg's theory of stages of moral development. Although he made universal claims, Kohlberg based his theory only on interviews with boys and men. He later "tested" girls and women and found they took longer than males to proceed through his six developmental stages. Gilligan asked if women and girls might not have a different conception of self and morality and explored that possibility by interviewing them about moral dilemmas in abortion. Gilligan found that concepts of responsibility and care are central to women's construction of the

Presented at the Michigan Department of Mental Health Women's Task Force Public Forum, "An Overview of Women's Mental Health Problems," Lansing, Michigan, September 19, 1980.

Dr. Thorne is a sociologist, on the faculty at Michigan State University, whose research has focused on gender differences.

45

moral domain, a type of moral sensibility neglected by Kohlberg, who emphasized conflicts of rights.

Feminist theorists have made other exciting contributions to our understanding of women's psychological development; for example, in gender organization and personality development (Chodorow, 1978; Dinnerstein, 1976); women and anger (Bernardez, 1978); and women's experiences and personal conflicts (Miller, 1976). These writings suggest that questions of boundaries and relations with others are central to women's experiences of self and the world, including their inner conflicts. For example, daughters sometimes fear that they lack autonomy and are only an extension of their mothers. Nancy Chodorow (1978) has examined gender asymmetries in development to study the boundary problem. She theorizes that because primary parenting is allocated to women, female children differentiate less sharply from their mothers and develop a relational personality structure, defining themselves in connection with others. This entails both strengths and problems. On the one hand, compared with men (whose personalities are more boundaried and agentic), women may have more empathy, capacity for intimacy, and awareness of their own emotions. On the other hand, they may be excessively preoccupied with the needs of others and have difficulty finding autonomy.

This is obviously an over-simplified summary of a complex theory. It is also over-generalized, for although gender is a central organizing principle in our society, there is wide individual variation in personality. There are also significant differences among women, and among men, related to race, ethnicity, social class, affectional preference, and age. It is important to learn more about these variations, while not losing sight of the contours of gender.

But, for all of the variation, there are dramatic patterns which point to the importance of social structure in creating separate fates for men and women. Many of these patterns are quickly summarized by a rule of thumb: the higher, the fewer. In every institution—hospitals, universities, professions, corporations, government agencies—the higher one goes in positions of power and opportunity, the fewer women and minorities are found. This is one side of the sexual division of labor: men have more access than women to public resources such as income, education, and political power. And minority women bear a double burden, disadvantaged both by race and by gender.

On the other side of the sexual division of labor, women have more responsibility than men for the daily tasks of caring for others—infants and children, the elderly, and other members of a household. Women not only do the bulk of housework and child-care, even when they are employed full-time; they are also dispro-portionately found in service jobs which extend maternal roles, such as nursing, social work, elementary teaching, secretarial work, and food serving.

One of the tragic features of the caregiving work of women, at home and in the workplace, is that it is socially devalued. "Women's work," more often than "men's work," is low paid and dead-end. Poverty is rapidly becoming "feminized," with the me-dian annual income of women workers still only 59% that of men, and with a dramatic increase in the percentage of women supporting households and of elderly women living alone. Women are often in hierarchical situations where they are subordinate and relatively powerless. This is true both in the world of paid work and in fami-lies.

Adrienne Rich (1977) has written of the poignant conjunction of powerlessness and power in women's experiences of mothering. On the one hand, mothers have power in bringing up and caring for in-fants and children. But motherhood is not a truly respected occupa-tion (if it were, why would women find themselves saying "I'm just a housewife"?), and mothers often work in conditions of economic deprivation, isolation, and disrespect.

While there is a popular view that heterosexual relationships are becoming more egalitarian, in fact, there is ample evidence of gender inequality in families. Men's greater power is evident of pro-cesses of family decision making, and in the prevalence of wife beating. The power of parents over children, and of husbands over wives, is ultimately backed by force. The least powerful members of families—children and women—are the most likely to be victims of violence (see Breines and Gordon, 1983; and Thorne and Yalom, 1982).

There is also evidence of greater male power in daily speech and communication between men and women. In mixed-sex conversa-tions, men interrupt women more than vice versa. One study found men interrupted women 96% of the time; another found men inter-rupted 75% of the time (West and Zimmerman, 1983). When women and men talk together, men also tend to control conversa-tional topics. Pamela Fishman (1978) analyzed 52 hours of taped conversation of three heterosexual couples at home. She found that while women brought up nearly two-thirds of all of the topics, their topics were rarely developed. When men raised a topic, conversation more often ensued. This was mostly because women did more of the "interaction work" of asking questions and providing verbal support. Note, once again, that it is women who do more caregiving; Fishman calls this "conversational housework."

The interaction patterns Fishman describes can be taken as a microcosm of asymmetric relationships between women and men. Men are more often the center of attention and in control of situations, and women more often attend to the needs of others, doing more of the invisible and unsung work of maintenance and caring. This division of tasks and values poses a complex challenge for those of us who seek to transform gender arrangements. It is obvious that we need to work to end women's subordination. Women have a right, and a need, to claim more power and resources, to gain full access to the public world and empowerment in daily interactions.

In over a decade of college teaching, I have observed that young women, more often than young men, seem deprived of two qualities: spiritedness, and the capacity to take themselves seriously. Women with this deprivation are often very nice; they are smiling, quiet, cooperative. The tragedy is hidden, and passive traits may even be rewarded. These are the types of women whom male therapists, for example, often like to have as patients and whom elementary school teachers reward for docility.

I believe that in our teaching, therapy, parenting, and other arenas of change, we should try to foster spiritedness in girls and women, helping them retain and develop a sense of seriousness and weight in the world. But in sorting out our long-range goals, we should be wary of a number of pitfalls which I will illustrate by a brief discussion of assertiveness training.

Assertiveness training is often presented as a way of helping women take themselves, and be taken, seriously; to transform the uncertainty and silence of women; and to give them tools to claim more verbal and interactional space. However, when the problem is seen as women's silence and lack of assertion, rather than men's control of women, the focus is one-sided. If women use more uncertain and hesitating speech, it may be because they are differentially interrupted and ignored. To focus only on women is to blame the victim. We also need to understand, and to change, men's control of women's talk and behavior. Furthermore, if we describe women's speech simply as unassertive, we may ignore its strengths. The supportive listening, self-disclosure, respect for others' turns, and "interaction work' which have been found in studies of talk among women (Thorne, Kramarae, and Henley, 1983) are weak or "powerless" only when contrasted with their opposites. For example, being sensitive to others' needs—inviting them to take turns at talk, drawing out the topics they raise—is heard as ineffectual only when this sensitivity is not reciprocated. These are patterns which men should learn; "empathy training" for men may be as needed as "assertiveness training" for women.

Other examples of blaming the victim can be found in notions such as "women's fear of success" (an idea with weak research support, which deflects attention from structural obstacles to women's advancement and achievement) and the "battered women syndrome" (which ignores women's economic dependence on men, the absence of felt alternatives to a particular home situation, and pressures toward heterosexuality).

I believe that although we want to overcome our positions of subordination and re-empower ourselves, we should not blindly accept the values built into the public world. Our challenge is not just to claim public power, but to transform it, to challenge its individualistic, competitive, and hierarchical assumptions. Women's experiences of caregiving and their values of cooperation and nurturance can provide a critique of the dominant institutions of society, which often deny human values. While we want to extricate women from subordination, we should also acknowledge and build upon "womanly" strengths of empathy and caregiving, and seek to make these more fully, and truly valued *human* qualities, embodied by both women and men.

FOOTNOTES

1. Carol Gilligan, "In a Different Voice: Women's Conception of the Self and of Morality," *Harvard Educational Review, 47* (4), 1977, pp. 481-517.
2. Nancy Chodorow, *The Reproduction of Mothering.* Berkeley, Calif.: University of California Press, 1978.
3. Dorothy Dinnerstein, *The Mermaid and the Minotaur.* New York: Harper & Row, 1976.
4. Teresa Bernardez, "Women and Anger: Conflicts with Aggression in Contemporary Women," *Journal of the American Medical Women's Association, 33,* May 1978, pp. 215-219.
5. Jean Baker Miller, *Toward a New Psychology of Women.* Boston: Beacon Press, 1976.

6. Adrienne Rich, *Of Woman Born: Motherhood as Experience and Institution.* New York: Bantam, 1977.

7. Don Zimmerman and Candace West, "Sex Roles, Interruptions and Silences in Conversation," in Barrie Thorne and Nancy Henley (eds.), *Language and Sex: Difference and Dominance.* Rowley, Mass.: Newbury House, 1975, pp. 105-125.

8. Pamela Fishman, "Interaction: The Work Women Do," *Social Problems, 25,* 1978, pp. 397-406.

Women in Inpatient Facilities: Impressions and Reflections

Eileen G. Thompson

The problems faced by women in state inpatient psychiatric facilities became real to me when I conducted a detailed review of inpatient records in one institution as part of a 1980 evaluation study of patient careers. Because of our small sample, it was not possible to document statistically differences between men and women in terms of admission and discharge criteria or treatment differences. However, based on my impressions, I found striking differences. I will present these differences as hypotheses, with the hope that in the future they may be tested with a thorough review. My conclusions concern what might be thought of as acute cases—"model clients" with only one or two inpatient episodes, hospitalized for less than 90 days.

Three women clients stand out particularly as typifying the problems I observed in the record review. Perhaps the single overall impression I gained was that these women were not permitted to define *for themselves* the nature of their problems, although they were more likely than men to admit that problems existed. The women talked about their problems according to the *structure* of their lives. In many cases, they talked to staff about making major changes in their lifestyle—leaving their husbands, being independent of their relatives, finding a job and achieving financial independence. Their families, on the other hand—whether involved in voluntary or involuntary admissions—defined the patients' problems strictly in terms of their mental or "nervous" condition. On the whole, the hospital staff seemed to concur with the family's definitions initially, and to persist in this way of viewing the clients even when their behavior

Dr. Thompson is a psychologist working as a research supervisor for Quaker Oats Company, Marketing Information Division. This research was conducted under the auspices of the Michigan Department of Mental Health.

51

was inconsistent with the initial diagnosis. For instance, there was a striking incidence of statements by the patients indicating a desire to leave their husbands and/or to separate from other family members. The patient presented this as a goal and a focal problem from the time of the intake interview. However, in each of the cases, no attempts were made to help or to support the patient in attaining this goal. Instead, the patient was encouraged to attempt to stay in the family situation and "work on it." This occurred even in the face of persistent resistance on the part of the other family members to participate in counseling or to work with the hospital staff on changing conditions within the family. Over a period of time, the patients apparently were affected by a positive contrast effect: in comparison to the hospital, going back to the family/spouse didn't look so bad. They were released back to the family—in several cases, to the husband's "custody," and in one case, with disastrous results.

There were several other hypotheses which the cases generated. Again, while they cannot be fully substantiated, they do seem worthy of discussion. First, it appears that the criteria for women to enter inpatient treatment may be looser than for men. This may be purely a result of women's willingness to seek help and admit problems before they result in severely disturbed behavior. It may also be a result of a broadening of the definition of "inability to care for self" to "inability to care for self or others for whom one is responsible."

Second, for women living in a family situation, there seems to be a tendency to set up post-hospitalization services in terms of individual or family therapy, rather than the more organized aftercare experiences involving day treatment services. Perhaps this is a result of the women's general level of functioning or perhaps it is a general practice for patients of both sexes who have families to return to. In any case, it seems that the aftercare services offered to these women reinforce their isolation from the community and their dependence on family members.

The first case typifying these problems was a middle-aged woman who had been married for a number of years and who did not work outside the home. She had been seeing a therapist for some time and was a voluntary admission to the facility, based on his recommendation. The presenting problem was obsessional behavior. In particular, when she was under stress she found it impossible to throw anything away and became compulsive about saving and organizing all the household trash. The formal problem list indicated that she had been suffering from auditory and visual hallucinations, but there was no record of any hallucinatory behavior in the ward notes.

This woman indicated to the hospital staff that her most serious problems involved her relationship with her husband. She stated that they had never really loved each other and had not been close for a number of years. She felt that he criticized her constantly and that the criticism left her "feeling paralyzed." She told the staff that she wanted very much to leave her husband and make a life for herself, but that she did not know what alternatives were available at her age. She had tried to take some college courses but had found herself very fearful and had to stop. The symptoms she described were similar to agoraphobia. She indicated a need for job-related counseling.

During her hospitalization, this woman did very well on the ward. She was pleasant and helpful to staff and other patients. Leaves of absence precipitated problems. Whenever she was scheduled to go home on leave, she became very depressed and frightened, expressing fears that she would do "something wrong" and talking about her worthlessness. Early in the episode, she continued to say that she did not want to return to her husband. After several weeks, she stopped expressing these feelings but was still depressed and apprehensive about the leaves.

After slightly more than a month of treatment with anti-anxiety medication, the hospital decided she was ready to leave. No discussions concerning her problems with her marriage were recorded. She was released to her husband to return home and continued to see the same therapist she had seen previously. The feelings and fears she had expressed to the ward staff about her marriage and independence and her desire for job training were not addressed in treatment or in discharge planning. Neither was her agoraphobia. Whether this woman will return to the hospital for future episodes may not be predictable. But the likelihood that her problems of feeling worthless and dependent and her fears of taking action in the world will continue can probably be predicted quite accurately.

The second female "model client" was a woman who showed very few signs of mental illness. Her primary problem was a group of relatives who developed a story that quite effectively made her look ill. In this case, it became clear that over time, the hospital staff began to see the true picture. It is doubtful that this woman should ever have been hospitalized.

She was an older woman, very recently widowed, with an elderly mother and a daughter and several nieces who expressed a great deal of concern about her behavior. She was a voluntary admission, diagnosed initially as a paranoid schizophrenic. The presenting problems included auditory hallucinations, decreased contact with and hostile behavior toward relatives, wandering away from home, and irresponsible behavior regarding the money from the probate of her husband's will. Once again, there was no evidence whatsoever of hallucinations in the ward notes. Moreover, the "wandering away from home" consisted of an apparently quite conscious decision to avoid her family by checking into a motel for a brief period of time.

During the month she was hospitalized, the records indicated that the staff began to see her "paranoid" behavior and hostility toward her family as fully justified. A fair amount of staff time was spent retrieving this woman's credit cards from the relatives, who were using them quite freely. Moreover, it became clear during therapy that the patient had not been irresponsible with money willed to her by her husband. In fact, she had received far less money than her relatives believed, because he had willed a large amount of money to someone else. The patient had not known about his relationship to this person until her husband's death, and she did not wish to reveal this information to her family.

During the inpatient episode, this patient too was helpful to patients and staff. She helped others with their laundry and did a great deal of crocheting. She commented to staff members that she felt she could handle things pretty well as long as she wasn't constantly having to deal with her family. She was placed on psychotropic medications, referred to psychotherapy and discharged.

The third case presented the most dramatic example of the problems outlined above. This woman was hospitalized under a court order because of violence toward her husband and inability to care for her child. The hospital psychiatrist and judge agreed that she was not mentally ill but that hospitalization would help her social adjustment. The woman had a history of episodes of hospitalization. She was highly religious, and through a number of episodes it was unclear whether her behavior was "crazy" or religiously based.

The precipitating incident to the hospitalization was the patient returning home with her new baby. She asked her husband to help cook the meals and, according to him, didn't pick up after herself. He labeled her behavior as "demanding." In the resulting argument, she threw a can of food at him. This, plus the fact that she woke the baby to nurse it, led him to seek institutionalization. She was hospitalized briefly at a private psychiatric facility, and caused great problems by insisting on continuing to breastfeed her baby. The staff responded by refusing to allow her to see the baby. Her angry behavior at this resulted in her transfer to the state facility.

The court petition for institutionalization stated that she was regarded as potentially dangerous to the baby. At first, the staff records supported this—it was reported that when her husband brought the baby in, she screamed at it. When someone heard this who understood Spanish, it was noted that the patient was screaming at the baby's *bottle,* not at the baby. Nursing the baby remained an issue while the patient was hospitalized. She clearly had very strong feelings about wanting to nurse the child. Facility staff told her that it would be unsafe for her to do so, because of the medications she was taking. The pharmacist's records, however, indicated that she had received only a single sleeping pill one evening and no other medications. Later, the staff forbade the breastfeeding based on facility schedules and procedures. The arguments over feeding the baby remained a major focus of the staff's attention.

Throughout the early period of hospitalization, the patient indicated that she wished to leave her husband and return to live with her parents. Near the end of her stay, her husband consented to become involved in therapy. She made the decision to go back to him and was discharged.

I would not make the charge here that facility staff directly emphasized saving these marriages. The willingness of patients who initially wish to leave their husbands to change their minds may result from a number of factors: a) compared to the hospital, problems at home don't seem as bad; b) during visits and leaves of absence, both individuals may be making special efforts and the problem areas of everyday life are not as salient; c) both individuals may be willing to try therapy and be hopeful about the outcome, with the willingness and hope fading later. However, the past history of these relationships suggests that the probability of finding solutions to the marital problems was not high. Perhaps the facility staff was simply overly optimistic about the potential results of the family therapy.

In this last case, the patient's decision to return to her husband ended tragically. Several weeks after her discharge, she was readmitted based on a number of psychotic symptoms. At the facility, she admitted that she had faked these symptoms in order to ask for help. The week before, her husband had beaten her and had taken the baby and had not returned. She was seeking help in finding her baby. In this instance, another psychiatrist was called in, and the patient was released for failure to certify. She was referred to legal aid. There is no further information in the records about the outcome of her search for the child.

Are there factors about these three cases and the others reviewed that are "typical" of the way women are dealt with in inpatient care? The report of the APA Task Force on outpatient care and the case studies they present corroborate these conclusions. However, without more extensive study, at present, we can only speculate. Hopefully, these issues will retain their importance to be the subject of research at some future time.

Women and Mental Health:
A Community Viewpoint

Rosalie Novara

When I was asked to address experiences of women in the community mental health system, I met with a number of women and men in my community who carry the labels, "patient," "therapist," "client," "case manager," and "parent." I asked them is there a different standard of mental health for men and women, how are women who enter the system treated and is community mental health sexist? They very generously shared their pain, frustration, humor, forgiveness and a delightful sense of the absurd. The richness of the experiences they shared with me and with each other goes far beyond my skills to communicate. They hoped that the pain of reliving and retelling their stories would help other women. Through our discussions, I tried to get a definitive answer, at least for our community, on whether the mental health system treats women differently from men. I found *three* definitive answers: yes, no, and maybe. There was great diversity on this topic, ranging from a solid opinion that women are engaged in a class upheaval and community mental health's role has been to suppress that struggle, to the more optimistic (?) point of view that the community mental health system oppresses women and men equally! On the other hand, no one offered the opinion that we are doing well with any of the people who came to us for help.

Is there a different standard of mental health for women and men? While answers varied, there was a general consensus that women's lives are very different from men's. In the past, role expectations

Presented at the DMH Women's Task Force Public Forum on "Treatment of the Female Client–Part I," Detroit, Michigan, January 16, 1981.

Rosalie Novara is a Masters level Social Worker, Assistant Director of the Kalamazoo County Community Mental Health Board, Kalamazoo, Michigan.

57

for a woman included responsibility for home management and for meeting the emotional needs of the family. The combined influence of feminism and economic pressure has meant that in over half of American families, the women's employment and income have become essential to the family's economic viability. However, as we all know, in many of these families there has been no commensurate sharing of women's original jobs. Many women carry a double burden. Reports of women entering the mental health system more frequently may not indicate emotional weakness but instead, suggest that women are so exhausted by meeting other people's needs and multiple role expectations that they do not have time to take care of their own physical, spiritual and emotional selves. They are used up. They continue to give, to perform, to produce with little support, long beyond the point that is healthy and reasonable. Men take their needs for nurturance and emotional support to their wives. Women do not have wives. They must go outside the family for assistance with emotional needs.

These statements are not meant to suggest that men do not have life pressures and role adjustment difficulties, but that men's and women's life experiences are different and the reasons for entering the mental health system are different as well.

Let me offer one example. A couple recently seen by a crisis worker were requesting voluntary state hospital admission for the woman. She was a woman in her 30s, a nurse with a demanding hospital job that she did well. But, while she was working full-time, she still retained total responsibility for the home even though others in the family were capable of sharing household tasks. She was depressed, exhausted and felt she could not go on. Her job performance was suffering. Her husband was supportive and caring in his way: he felt badly that she wasn't coping better. Neither of them saw any way out or any way for things to be different because of their inbred sense of appropriate roles. Needless to say, we did not recommend admission. Crisis services were focused on getting her the rest she needed for some time while other family members worked on splitting up the household tasks.

However, as recently as five years ago, this woman would have been admitted and convinced that she was emotionally ill. How typical this is, I cannot say. Most of the women I spoke with who were survivors of the bad old days at the state hospitals felt that men are allowed a wider range of aggressive and acting out behaviors before being considered deviant or threatening.

How do we treat women who enter the system? Again, people's impressions are scattered and diverse. We have heard many stories of abuse, brutalization and degradation in the hospital, most of them taking place before the new Mental Health Code (1974), but some more recently. However, most of the women I spoke with thought that men had been equally frequently abused, neglected or brutalized. The constant danger of reinforcing dependent behavior in the name of treatment seems to be a problem that occurs for both men and women in the hospital *and* the community. Women reported many instances of appropriate assertive behavior eliciting negative, punitive responses: Women questioning the side effects of medication have been told that they are hostile and resistive to treatment. Genuine healthy expressions of anger were called hysteria and cured with large doses of Stellazine. Many women reported feeling especially powerless with psychiatrists. "When women rely too much on the ideas of doctors," one said, "it shows that we don't have faith in ourselves. Why do we let men tell us what to do?"

One indication of how women are treated is recipient rights complaints. In Kalamazoo County, numbers of complaints from women and men are about equal and there is little difference by type of complaint. The one exception is in the area of being treated with dignity and respect. Many more women than men complain that they are treated rudely or in a humiliating way. Almost invariably, these complaints are filed against psychiatrists, mostly men, or clerical/reception staff who are predominantly women.

Most of the real horror stories that I have heard have taken place in institutions. For instance, one psychiatrist whose treatment of choice for women in the hospital was hysterectomies. He seemed to feel that regardless of age, every crazy woman would do better without her womb. This physician now practices privately and hasn't given up on this idea. While he can no longer coerce women into having hysterectomies, I am told he still makes his pitch to his private clients.

Another psychiatrist, a charming fellow, has excellent clinical skills and does very well with both men and women. Unfortunately, using his charm is part of his treatment plan for many of the women he sees. Women say he runs a vicious game. He encourages women to become emotionally attached, then if their attachment becomes a problem for him or if the woman herself tries to break off the emotional relationship, he becomes punitive. He may persuade the family that the woman needs electroshock therapy. In one case, I was told, a lobotomy was performed. Unfortunately, none of the women involved have ever been willing to pursue a court case.

In response to the question, *Is treatment in community mental health sexist?,* the answer overwhelmingly given was "Of course!, how could it not be? Our whole society is sexist!" Many male therapists (and some women) seem to feel most comfortable following traditional male roles with their female clients. Frequently mentioned are the roles of father or lover. The therapist who takes the father role may be protective ("Poor lady, let me take care of your problems for you."). This protectiveness may turn into pushiness, with an impatience for the years and centuries of conditioning and guilt that keeps a woman in an untenable situation. He may become hostile or rejecting when his suggestions for change aren't followed by immediate action.

The therapist who takes the male role of lover is like the psychiatrist described above. He may not carry it to such vicious extremes, yet does foster an emotional dependence, a flirtatiousness or sexual excitement that sometimes encourages a woman to end her marriage in the hopes of more exciting prospects elsewhere.

Another area of sexism involves vocational assessments and rehabilitation programs. Some staff in these programs still seem to believe that any woman whose hands are not crippled should be trained as a secretary. We have lots of work to do here.

The parent role presents a special set of problems. Perhaps you have seen this bumper sticker, "Mental illness is catching. You get it from your kids." One study we did seemed to corroborate this connection. In a random sample of over a thousand households, a much higher percentage of people who had sought community mental health services were parents than those who had never had contact with the system. The problems that occur for parents of the handicapped are even greater. The mother is almost always the person who approaches the system for help. The child's label might be Mentally Ill, Developmentally Disabled or Learning Disabled. The mother's label might be "overprotective," "controlling," "hysterical," or "overemotional."

Parents experience so much guilt when there is a problem with a child. Women often experience more guilt because of their greater involvement in the child's development. They feel especially vulnerable to judgmental reactions of professionals. Most women parents feel their knowledge is discounted. It is infuriating, they say, to have their opinions ignored for weeks, then to see a professional listen eagerly to the comments of their husband who is involved only sporadically. If it is any comfort to us, most parents report that community mental health is not nearly as bad as the school system.

Lack of understanding of women's menstrual cycles and birth control have also contributed to misdiagnosis and mislabeling that is sexist. From the stories I have heard, the interaction between physical and emotional factors is very poorly understood. Reactions to birth control pills are an example. One woman told the story of becoming suicidal after starting on the pill. Until she stopped taking the pill for other reasons and her depression lifted, neither she, her doctor, nor her therapist recognized that her "emotional illness" was physically (hormonally) induced.

Another woman told the story of going off the pill after taking it for many years. The pill had suppressed the emotional fluctuations connected with her menstrual cycle. When she went off the pill, the extremes of her ups and downs were frightening to her and she sought counseling. It was a year before she figured out that she was reacting in a new way to her menstrual cycle.

There is a trap in this. Women have been told for years that they don't belong in the workplace because they are at the mercy of their hormones. Most of us who experience monthly ups and downs can cope with them. Some women experience more severe reactions and don't get much help from the medical or mental health systems. One woman told the story of being unable to control fear and anxiety on certain days. This did present problems at work. On her own, she established that these days always came just before her periods. Unfortunately, her periods were unpredictable and she never knew when one of those days would happen. Her medical doctor sent her to a psychiatrist. The psychiatrist's solution was for her to quit her job.

When women are treated with tranquilizers or psychotropics in situations like these, the problems become compounded. Menstrual cycles become abnormal and the woman's usual physical/emotional balance or imbalance gets turned around. We need to know much more about women and emotional and physical cycles and interactions and cannot let ourselves be frightened off by charges that our hormones rule us.

I have highlighted some of the problems that are played out in unique ways for women. I would now like to return to the point made near the beginning—perhaps the mental health system oppresses men and women equally. The overwhelming impression I received from all my conversations was that while all of the above are problems, the mental health system has serious problems that go beyond the boundaries of male/female. One is the problem of diagnoses and labels and the other is the inadequate resources we have to help people get better.

Putting labels on people stifles and kills potential for growth. A "psychiatric diagnosis" tells us nothing and allows us to react to people as "schizophrenics" or "hysterics" instead of unique individuals worthy of individual consideration.

The strongest feelings that have been expressed to me have been the pain of misdiagnoses, rediagnoses and differential staff response by diagnosis. This is perceived as a major cause of dehumanization in our system.

The other point made very strongly is that a client's personal potential for growth, change and wellness is great. Our skills at helping are limited and we do not have anywhere near the amount of resources we need to do the intense work necessary with people who are desperate for help. This is not to say that attention to the problems outlined above as unique to women is not required. Much more information, sensitivity, and skill are needed. But we also have to recognize that we have wider problems and, according to the women I spoke with, these wider problems, the hazards of labeling and the limited availability of good therapy, are the major challenges to be faced by the community mental health system.

Sexual Exploitation
of Clients by Therapists

Gary Schoener
Jeanette Hofstee Milgrom
John Gonsiorek

In 1974, Walk-In Counseling Center (WICC) of Minneapolis began providing counseling, support and advocacy services for clients who alleged sexual involvement with past or current psychotherapists. Since then, WICC has handled over 250 cases in various capacities. In 1976-1977, one of us (J.M.) co-led a group for female victims and in 1980, assisted staff at Family and Children's Services of Minneapolis in developing the first of a series of similar groups (Luepker and Retsch-Bogart, 1980). We have also provided consultation to agencies to prevent the occurrence and/or cope with the aftermath of a staff member's sexual exploitation of clients. After briefly reviewing the literature, we will describe common client responses and suggest clinical and advocacy interventions. As information and data in this area are limited, our descriptions are impressionistic and approximate, and should be viewed as working hypotheses and tentative suggestions, *not* as facts. As most victims are women, female pronouns are used throughout this paper.

INTRODUCTION

Reports in the literature on client-therapist sexual involvement are sparse and also limited in methodology and professional discipline (psychiatry and psychology). Overall, between 15% and 16%

Gary Schoener is a licensed psychologist and Executive Director of the Walk-In Counseling Center, Inc. (WICC), Minneapolis since 1973; Jeanette H. Milgrom, MSW, is Director of Consultation and Training at WICC; and John Gonsiorek, PhD, is Director of Psychological Services at Twin Cities Therapy Clinic, Minneapolis and previous Clinic Director at WICC.

of male therapists and 2% and 3% of female therapists admit to
erotic contact with clients (Kardener, Fuller, and Mensh, 1973;
Holroyd and Brodsky, 1977). Since these figures are entirely based
on *therapist* self-report, they can be safely assumed to represent
minimal estimates of incidence. (Asking psychiatrists if they *knew*
of others' sexual involvement, one study reported 50% knew of
cases, even though most had not reported this; Grunebaum, Nadelson, and Macht, 1976.) There are also case reports of sexual harassment and abuse by clergy (Rassieur, 1976) and paraprofessionals
(Schoener, 1974). The most likely victim is clearly female and the
exploiter male (Belote, 1974; D'Addario, 1977) although there may
be more variation in the latter.[*] There is also some suggestion that
most therapists sexually involved with clients have done so repeatedly (median = 6; mean = 29 times according to Holroyd and
Brodsky, 1977).

There is a growing professional literature on client/therapist sexual involvement (Eigen, 1973; Hare-Mustin, 1974; Edelwich and
Brodsky, 1982). The methodology of intervention in such cases is
now also beginning to be identified (Fleming, Luepker, Nye, and
Schoener, 1982; Gonsiorek, 1984; Luepker and Retsch-Bogart,
1980; Milgrom, 1981; Schoener, 1979; Schoener, Milgrom, and
Gonsiorek, 1983). However, surveys of victims are lacking.

COMMON CLIENT REACTIONS TO SEXUAL EXPLOITATION BY THERAPISTS

1. *Guilt and Shame:* Most clients slip into a posture common to
victims—blaming themselves. Guilt may center on feelings of being
seductive or ruining the therapist's life or career, etc. Some clients
are so obsessed with guilt as to ignore the professional therapist's
responsibility to provide treatment and act in the client's best interest. Many therapists are masters of guilt induction and/or of getting
clients to protect them. Some clients are so intrapunitive that their
experience of guilt/shame can last for months or even years.

2. *Grief:* Whether the client or therapist breaks it off, grief reactions over loss of a significant love relationship often ensue. The

---

[*]Of WICC's 250 cases, 30 involved female/female involvement. Given the low base rates
for lesbianism, this is surprising. That only four cases have involved male client/female
therapist probably is not, since it may be more difficult for a male to see himself victim to a
female. Eight cases involved male/male involvement.

longer and more intense the relationship, the more intense the grief. Some clients are unable to handle this grief and refuse to separate from the therapist.

3. *Anger/Rage:* The client may feel angry about many things: violation of trust; exploitation; being deprived of much-needed therapy during a vulnerable period; leaving therapy worse off than before because of the new burden of confusion/guilt/shame; wasting a critical period in one's life on a relationship which couldn't last; the therapist setting up all the rules and successfully controlling her, etc. Many feel especially angry that the power differential continues even after therapy terminates: either as an unresolved personal issue or because filing a complaint can lead to another ordeal.

4. *Depression and Loss of Self-Esteem:* Depression and low self-esteem are two of the most common problems which lead people to seek therapy. Sexual exploitation by the therapist typically exacerbates these problems. Persistent guilt feelings or anger turned inward as a result of exploitation can even *create* depression and self-esteem problems where they did not exist before.

Some exploitive therapists interpret a client's unwillingness to initially become sexually involved as an "inability to love" or to "trust" and "accept love." The client's anxiety about intimacy with the therapist is interpreted as further evidence of neurosis. Even after termination, clients may feel badly about not having been able to accept the love of the therapist. Other clients may be angry at themselves for being vulnerable and trusting. Many do not even give themselves credit for having pulled out of the relationship, but rather continue to put themselves down for having ever succumbed.

In the course of therapy, some clients improve their self-concept via identification with the therapist. The client's personal values may shift toward those of the therapist. Even in an exploitive situation, some of these values and the personal changes made are quite healthy ones. In an attempt to rid herself of the connection with the exploitive therapist, the client may try to reject healthy changes.

5. *Ambivalence and Confusion:* Persons entering therapy typically have confused feelings and look to therapy for reality-testing. Sexual involvement with a therapist adds to this confusion and can lead to marked ambivalence and extreme mood swings as feelings come into conflict. For example, along with anger, many clients feel gratitude over positive aspects of therapy. Many want to see the therapist again to clear up this ambivalence or challenge him to explain his behavior. They wonder about: "Did he really care about

me?''; ''Is he sick—is he evil?''; ''Was I special, or were there others?''; ''Why me—what attracted him to me?'' Some clients are virtually certain that they were the only one, although in the vast majority of our cases this was not true. Clients sometimes become outraged and very *un*ambivalent when they learn they aren't ''special.''

6. *Fear:* Much like rape or incest victims, many clients fear rejection by spouses, lovers, family, and the community at large for having been involved in an illicit sexual relationship. Many fear expressing their anger, expecting that they will be labeled ''castrating'' or vindictive or not be believed, or that others will be less likely to help them. Many clients are fearful of ruining the therapist's career or of his reaction to their reporting the abuse. The client needs reassurance that this is not her responsibility.

It should be noted, however, that in a minority of situations, therapists attempt to pressure clients who are complaining, and in a few, they enlist the aid of others in doing so, even going to the community in some cases.

7. *Massive Distrust:* Many clients find themselves very distrustful of therapists, or even males in general. Victims of male therapists may fear that even female therapists will breach trust or misuse power. Where the therapist has also violated other boundaries, such as confidentiality, the trust level may be even lower. This distrust can even generalize to old friends and family.

It is important to recognize, identify, and accept the client's distrust, to establish its parameters, and to commend her for being appropriately guarded. Even though we make it clear that we do not become sexually involved with clients and we carefully guard confidentiality, we do not expect to be trusted completely, nor is such trust necessary for us to be helpful. To invite expression of concern, confusion, or distrust, we periodically ask clients for feedback about our intervention and follow-up therapy. As many clients have come to distrust therapy (as a result of the violation of their boundaries by the therapist), we attempt to reduce expectations about therapy and focus on the client's own abilities to cope and change.

WORKING WITH VICTIMS OF SEXUAL EXPLOITATION BY THERAPISTS

1. *Don't make any assumptions about the sexual behaviors or verbal advances which occurred:* If and when the client is willing to discuss the sexual encounter, explore what specifically was in-

volved. Many sexual encounters with therapists do not involve intercourse, but involve kissing, breast or genital fondling (with or without orgasm), oral sex, anal sex, with either party playing various roles. Therapists may experiment with clients sexually, engaging in various acts atypical for them in other contexts.

2. *Don't make assumptions about how the sexual involvement affected the client:* Many clients have very ambivalent feelings about their sexual/romantic experience with a therapist. Don't expect consistency. Allow the feelings to unfold and do not force a resolution of mixed or confusing feelings. Try to give reassurance and permission to talk about the positive *and* negative feelings.

3. *Examine the nature of the relationship carefully:* Was this experienced by the client as a love affair, perhaps with meetings outside of the therapy sessions and promises of an ongoing affair or marriage; or was the sex introduced as a therapeutic technique? When and how did the romantic talk or sexualizing of the relationship begin? How did it develop? Words and fantasies are important guideposts. Seductiveness by the therapist, even if not acted upon, can be destructive or confusing.

4. *Explore how the client feels about seeing you:* Most clients are understandably cautious, fearful, and/or ambivalent about re-entering therapy. They feel violated and distrustful of therapists in general. State that you do not get romantically/sexually involved with clients and be clear about the limits you place on touching. Emphasize what she can do:

   a. question you if she doesn't agree or feels uncomfortable;
   b. request that you bring in a co-therapist or consultant; or
   c. request a referral to another therapist.

5. *Focus initial intervention on crisis issues:* First, is the client at risk, suicidal? Second, what real-life issues are facing the client including those related to complaints filed, planned confrontations with the therapist/relatives, etc.? Third, assist the client in dealing with emotional pain, grief, anger, feelings of victimization, etc. Any exploration of personality dynamics of the client can occur *later*.

6. *Do not further violate the client in the way you work with her:* All of the above suggestions are focused on the client's, not the helper's, needs taking precedence. The client has just emerged from a situation where her needs were exploitively subsumed to the therapist's. One of the most profound therapeutic interventions you can do is to consistently respect her needs and put them first. Do not let

your anger at the exploitive therapist or impatience at the victim's ambivalence or slow pace deflect you from this *most* basic point.

7. *Assist the client in exploring different avenues of complaint:* Clients vary from not having considered filing a complaint, to assuming that you will, to wanting specific help in doing so. It's important to be well-informed on the options available so that you can help the client explore them. WICC has a monograph which may help you do this (Schoener, 1979). It is noteworthy that in virtually all of our cases in which a complaint was made, the client and/or her significant others reported that the complaint was beneficial to resolving the experience.

8. *Support groups can be helpful:* While groups for victims of sexual exploitation are rare, a few support groups do exist. In their absence, a general women's group or consumer advocacy group may provide helpful support and validation.

9. *Consider a processing session with the therapist and client:* While a client's attorney or a licensure board may discourage this, we have found that a properly facilitated session with the client and abusing therapist can help restore the client's reality-testing and provide for useful ventilation of feelings. Some clients prefer to confront the therapist by themselves. In several instances, they have done this over the phone and taped it so it could be processed later. The authors are available for consultation prior to such an undertaking, having had an unusual amount of experience in this area.

CLOSING COMMENTS

Working with clients who have been sexually exploited by therapists is highly stressful. We have several suggestions for an effective program. First, a *team* of individuals involved in the case is highly recommended to prevent burn-out, and allow helpers to ventilate their frustrations to the team, instead of the client. A team approach allows for a division of labor by natural talents, e.g., to work with different types of victims and victimization, with the legal system, etc.

Second, the program should not hesitate to pressure professional organizations to develop an effective response. Ethics panels are often initially hesitant to handle these cases. However, time spent in lobbying, training, or educating may be well spent in eventually providing useful avenues of complaint or effective peer pressure for improvements.

Third and finally, program resources should be available to help develop a core of legal experts. For clients who decide to initiate legal action, strong collaborative working relationships with attorneys specializing in civil rights, mental health malpractice, etc., is invaluable to facilitate successful outcomes and increase the sophistication of all disciplines involved. A few successful lawsuits can provide a powerful adjunct to other persuasive techniques in getting professional associations to recognize and effectively fulfill their obligations to protect client welfare.

The Killing Ground:
Police Powers and Psychiatry

Kelli Quinn

I'm an ex-psychiatric inmate, and a very angry woman. I lost ten years of my life in mental "prisons." That's where the patriarchy places women who refuse to keep their place and reject male definitions of themselves. I couldn't see myself through the eyes of men, and was punished as "crazy" because I couldn't adjust myself to their line of vision.

I don't see things their way. Sorry.

I'm a member of the Psychiatric Alternatives Alliance, an ex-inmate activist group whose sole purpose for existing is to destroy the name "crazy," and the psychiatric industry which profits so much from its existence!

I want to share with my sisters on the Women's Task Force a story about the terrible things that can happen when women use psychiatry to "help" each other, and it seems to be happening more and more.

Psychiatry is male, and it benefits all men in power. It cripples and kills. The only way that women can and do use it, is against each other. This happened one summer, at the Michigan Womyn's Music Festival, on all-woman ground and all-woman space. Psychiatry is so powerful that 10,000 women could not prevent one "crazy" woman in their midst at the Festival from being locked up. Think about it, the next time you think we ought to use it.

To the producers of the Womyn's Music Festival:

I'm writing to share my pain and anger as a lesbian (ex)patient who attended this year's Festival in August.

I'm referring to the fact that we handed a sister over this summer.

Kelli Quinn is a member of Psychiatric Alternatives Alliance, a consumer group, and also serves on the gubernatorially-appointed Michigan Mental Health Advisory Council.

71

Armed to the teeth with misogynist ideas about our own suffering,
and falling back on the police powers of the State, we forcefully re-
moved a woman from our midst and handed her over to the shrinks!

It's the bitterest irony to me, that she was "helped" off the land
and into their clutches by a psychiatric nurse and woman shrink.
How pitifully damning, that the shrinks saw no business in her to
treat.

We were good little girls running to Papa. If there was any way
he could have scooped one of us up, he would have. Because Psychiatry is business. Big business.

It's got nothing to do with taking care of people, and everything to
do with institutionalized prejudice masquerading as medical opinion.

I don't say this to obscure the reality that we were doing the best
we could with the energy and understandings we had at the time. I
say it to point out the larger realities about how we were acting on
assumptions and priorities that did desperate violence to the woman
involved and each of use who participated. And I contend that we all
participated. . .all are responsible.

To know that this happened, and to know that some of us are nam-
ing our helping "Psychiatry," is absolutely frightening. It says
we've bought into the language and laws of our own oppression, and
that we're desperately out of touch with it.

For many of us, our choice to give our energies totally to wimmin
breaks patriarchal law. Yet we used the privilege of that law—designed to protect property and exclude everything else but the white
man—to deprive a sister of her choices and her freedoms.

We stripped the freedom from the hands of a sister without trial,
whose only crime was to suffer in a way that was unacceptable/un-
recognizable to us. And we remanded her to a profession that is the
epitomy of womon-hating. One that, until recently, had the lifestyle
many of us have chosen listed in its Diagnostic II Manual as a
"pathology."

Please recognize that the violence we did that womon was only
made possible by dubbing her "mental patient" material. To use the
same coercion on a medical patient, or any other womon who hadn't
first been tried and found guilty of a crime would be to commit assault and battery or even kidnapping. Mental patients have no rights.
I'm sorry we moved a sister down the road toward being one.

It makes no sense to argue that the womon struggled and then finally went willingly. The fact is that her options were chosen for her

by what we chose to name her suffering, and what we allowed her next hours to become.

And when we couldn't get a "quick fix," we left her in the town, until some others of us came to our senses and retrieved her.

Grabbing the legs of performers, you say? If the womon was hassling people, she should have been helped to "cool it," and if she couldn't, asked to leave the grounds until she could, with the same responsibilities and consequences as anyone else.

Coercion should never be an option! To think it's okay for certain (inferior) categories of wimmin is intolerable. And privatising wimmin's suffering IS DANGEROUS. It places it outside of life (which is the only place it belongs) and puts it in a place where the oppression operating in it can't be identified or dealt with.

We need a quiet, supportive place for wimmin who are struggling. It should be a part, and not a-part from the workings of the rest of the Festival, and it should have wimmin ex-patients and others constantly available to it who are sensitive to what "mentalist" sentencing and silencing are all about.

And as for sentences and silences, it was a bad thing, with lasting implications for the welfare of all of us, your refusal as producers to acknowledge what went down as a public threat to the Festival community, and to straightforwardly deal with the issues, feelings and alternatives it generated.

That womon was disrupting your business, and by God, you took care of her, didn't you?

I'm really angry that you could ask for more money to secure the Festival land, with less regard for the wimmin on it.

You said that the bottom line was that wimmin must feel safe. Well, that bottom line sure feels like business to me.

I was part of a workshop at the Festival on Wimmin in Prisons and Mental Institutions put out by the Womyn Free Womyn in Prison Collective. We learned of the women's situation, met with the Womb coordinator, drafted a collective statement to bring the situation to public attention, located the womon's friends, and brought her back to the land.

We thought there'd be no problem in getting you to bring it to public attention, and make a public commitment to our welfare. We decided I'd read the statement if that's what it came to. I say this not because that was important, but because the commitment on my part to read it, and/or see the issue outran myself and others up against the wall. And it was a HARD one.

What happened? We couldn't get the issue surfaced or a public commitment to solve it. It was stonewalled and silenced.

We realized the problem went beyond some consciousness-raising at the Womb medical tent. And I'm talking about more here than "policy" problems of "access" and "accountability." The terms are deceptive. They're system words, and that's ultimately what, and who, they serve and protect!

A lot of workers were put in the middle between legitimate needs and illegitimate priorities. And who put them there? You did. If you want the privilege of hierarchy, you also get the onions.

After hours of struggle, you send word that three of us (God knows we don't have time for all wimmin) be taken back into a tent to sit down with workers in an interchange that could do nothing else but violate both of us. Because the Great Sit-Down wasn't about our safety anymore. It was about yours, your needs and prerogatives.

It went like this: "The music's almost over, and if you want your statement out, you'll have to add to it, the (successful) process that is now taking place between the Festival staff and concerned Festival goers. (Screw that system name for us by now. . .we're ex-patients!) And incidentally, you can't go up on stage to read it by yourselves. Only staff can do that. Can we get a consensus on that? If we can't, it won't get read at all."

Exhausted by now, most of us give in, despairing. Ages pass as one strong womon down from me breaks the consensus again and again. . .

We ask that staff go up with one ex-patient and assist us in reading our own statement. "Sorry."

Finally, it comes down to myself and staff going up to share a statement that hides a lot. Wimmin are swarming around the table by this time, and refuse to "hive off."

We step out of the tent and a mass of workers, patients and other Festival wimmin tell us the same thing. Like, "We're all being screwed. You've got to go up there."

The staff comes out of the tent and tells us that we can go up with them, but they've decided by this time that we aren't to help with the statement.

I tell them I'll go, but under those circumstances, there's no way I'll keep my mouth shut. We leave for the stage. As we arrive, staff breaks rank with me. They refuse to let us up. They say we "can't be trusted."

I'll tell you honestly, I felt a lot of tenderness in that circle. And I felt a lot of goodwill getting its back broke because it could only be worded in, consensed upon, things that protected the system. If the system had worked, we wouldn't have been back in the tent in the first place.

I'm sending you the statement from the wimmin in the workshop. I hope you'll help us. If you're out to move the Festival toward something REAL for wimmin, there's a lot of us who'll burn heart and haul ass.

But if you're out to make Vogel Land off our backs, you're playing a dangerous game, cause ain't none of us wimmin stupid. We wouldn't have lived this long.

I hope I hear from you a commitment to struggle.

I'm struggling,
Kelli Quinn
Psychiatric Alternatives Alliance

STATEMENT

(Put out by the Womyn in Prisons and Mental Institutions Workshop, sponsored by Womyn Free Womyn in Prison Collective.)

Sisterhood is powerful, it can kill you.

A womon lost her freedom here today. She was acting in some ways that we couldn't handle and we took her out into the boy's world and handed her over to the shrinks!

This happens every year at the Festival. WE CANNOT LET IT HAPPEN AGAIN!

Putting somebody in a psychiatric institution is Michigan's answer to capital punishment. So many of our sisters die there.

We are frightened when we hear statements such as, "She was POTENTIALLY dangerous to herself and others." These are words that have been used to lock the doors behind many of our sisters!

We need to COLLECTIVELY set alternatives. Stop the violence committed against us by the criminal justice system, the psychiatric establishment.

We must refuse to let our sisters be locked up. Can you believe that you could come here and lose your shit and wind up in a mental institution?

We need a space, coordinated by ex-psychiatric inmates, where wimmin in crises can be safe and cared for 24 hours a day. We must guarantee that no womon ever be handed over!

We need a tent where ex-psychiatric and prison inmates can meet. We need a tent where lesbians who are in battering relationships can meet.

We need to recognize that the violence in our lives is real, even here at "Michigan," and that none of us is safe from it!

There is a lot of talking about sisterhood, but in the end, we are handing sisters over to the cops, shrinks, jails, prisons and institutions.

We are wimmin, emotional people, and this is a part of life and we have to deal with it.

Epilogue: I'm long past talking about his violence. I'm frightened of ours. The oppression women hand to each other. He's moved onto our ground. A bunch of you, inculcated in his prejudice, move before him. Women clinicians with his words in your mouths and his thoughts in your heads.

It all settles upon our backs, like radiation fallout. Some of us it kills right away. Others it kills slowly. And some of us survive.

So far, I've survived. He locked me up, ten years of my life, and I'm another ten getting over it.

I watch and listen to you, the Women of the Task Force, and I realize that we may never get over it. You've put his walls between us. I'm your token ex-nut. The one crazy woman you've asked to speak at a public forum on women's "treatment" issues. The voice of the rest of your sisters that you've silenced.

You don't realize our absence. Our presence is of lesser value than yours, the experts on the pain of other women, the crazy women.

We are things (as all women are things), talked about and acted upon, but one thing we can never do very well or very far is speak for ourselves.

We can't think about our situations. What we are, what we want, is flawed. There's something wrong with the way we suffer. His foot may be on our backs, but it hurts too much, and we're angry too long. You'd have us believe that there's a correct response to his oppression. A healthy way to suffer.

We don't need him on our backs. You're on them. Women keeping other women in line. Women saying what is good for other women. Women deciding now, who can think clearly and who can't. Who can benefit from therapeutic propaganda and who can't, and who should be forced for her own good and who can be counted on to submit voluntarily.

The same old killing paternalism. His rules and his terms. His games and his ground. Makes things of us. The nut needs the treatment. The object provokes its use. It justifies all that's done.

No one leaves the field. I'm safe now, but not for very far or very long. I survive but no one knows it. Plowed back into his field to fertilize his ground. Women who have survived the psychiatric industry aren't recognized and valued for what they are—survivors, oppressed, system abused. No. Name us "crazy," "chronically mentally ill."

Some of us must be above the others. Keeps no one sure of her ground. Apart and away from the others. No common ground.

You good little girls up there by Papa. He's lent you his power. Those of you he lets in power, have power to wield his prejudice. You name, define and discriminate. We need tighter diagnosis, you say. More appropriate use of behavior control drugs. What he names us, and what he does to us, even by force, is never done away with. It's just done more "appropriately."

And you speak about "prevention" strategies. Distinguish, divide and separate the real crazies from the women with problems. Let some of us off the hook, to keep the reality of the hook, and some of us, thrashing upon it.

You discriminate in the wrong places. Among us, rather than down the root and against him.

SECTION 3:
DIAGNOSES APPLIED TO WOMEN:
THE EVIDENCE

Example: Anorexia Nervosa

In western culture, a high value is placed on slenderness in women. The media is rife with overt and covert messages stressing its importance. Fashion is designed for the slender woman. Existing prejudice against obesity is further fueled by medical evidence that being overweight increases health risks and jeopardizes longevity. There are immense cultural pressures on women to achieve the ideal female body and some evidence of discrimination in jobs and college admission on the basis of weight (Brodsky and Hare-Mustin, 1980; Canning and Maya, 1966). Girls, even more than boys, are critical of obesity and of their own body image (Clifford, 1971; Jourard and Secord, 1955; Boskind-White and White, 1983).

Women are under constant pressure to change their bodies and, as a result, risk constant failure. This can be very damaging to self-esteem and so weight control is an important emotional issue for many women. Over the past ten years there seems to be increased pressure to diet, concern over weight control, and idealization of a thinner body size (e.g., Garner et al., 1980, who analyzed data on Miss America winners and contestants and *Playboy* centerfolds).

Anorexia nervosa is a severe problem of weight control in

which malnutrition and life-threatening weight loss occur because of caloric restriction that is psychologically-based—not related to poverty or the availability of food. Anorexics usually exhibit no loss of appetite (at least not until they enter the starvation phase of the illness). The main feature is, in fact, "a conflict between a frantic preoccupation with food and an active restraint from eating" (Al-Issa, 1980). The disorder is most prevalent in women 25 years or under and is most often characterized by "the relentless pursuit of a thin body size in spite of emaciation" (Garfinkel and Garner, 1982, p. 26). Although there is no single definition, specific other criteria for diagnosing the disorder usually include early onset, severe weight loss (e.g., 25%), and a *fear* of obesity.

It is also not clear whether certain features are part of the psychiatric disorder or are secondary to starvation and extreme weight loss. Some metabolic disturbances are directly related to degree of weight loss or caloric intake (such as thermoregulation, adrenal function, growth hormone, etc.). Most would agree that amenorrhea is the result of weight loss below a certain level critical for normal menstruation (fat levels below 22% of body weight), causing a regression to a prepubertal state. However, in a not insignificant proportion of cases (varying between 7% and 24%), amenorrhea appears to precede weight loss. The loss of menses may be due to psychiatric disturbance, emotional trauma or may be an independent hypothalamic abnormality. Most patients do resume menses with restoration of a minimum weight for height. Other relevant factors are percentage of body fat and removal of stress. The majority of recovered anorexics are reportedly normally fertile; however, pregnancy should be definitely avoided until recovery occurs (Garfinkel and Garner, 1982).

Many anorexic patients also experience hyperactivity and bloated sensations even after eating small quantities of food. Whether or not these are the results of starvation is not clear, since they do not appear in other cases of starvation and may be experienced independently of weight loss.

Anorexics tend to believe that their weight is normal, despite their slenderness. In fact, denial is a significant early feature in the disorder. Rigid eating habits are used to control weight sometimes accompanied by attempts to hide the extreme dieting behaviors. Other aspects of the syndrome include: a preoccupation with good and evil, rigid thinking, denial of all problems, sense of ineffectiveness, personal mistrust, anhedonia with an accompanying desire to live only in the mental sphere—overall, a split between mind and body with the former attempting to override and control the latter (Garfinkel and Garner, 1982).

Incident reports of anorexia nervosa in the general population vary from .37 per 1,000 to 7 per 100, depending on the population (Garfinkel and Garner, 1982; Kendall et al., 1973), higher among college students and psychiatric patients (McManus et al., 1982). Male to female ratios range from 1:14 to 1:24. Anorexia nervosa is usually thought to be associated with an over-affluent, overnourished society, explaining its prevalence among girls from the upper and middle classes (Corsp et al., 1976). Anorexia appears to be increasing in frequency, although this may be confounded with greater awareness of the disorder and consequently more accurate reporting. Along with this overall increased frequency, there appears to be a trend toward an increase in age of onset, a greater prevalence in older women, and a more even distribution throughout all social classes (Garfinkel and Garner, 1982).

In the psychodynamics of anorexia, success or failure at weight control is a "symbol" of the ability to control life in general. This success is experienced as a pleasure in disproportion to all physical and social benefits while failure is experienced as "profoundly demoralizing." Patients often feel terror about giving in to an impulse to eat. Weight control is an "important metaphor" in these women's lives. In fact, their fear causes avoidance of food which leads to a food preoccupation (induced by starvation) which further magnifies fears and causes greater eating restrictions (Brodsky and Hare-Mustin, 1980). Other psychological factors cited are stress associated with maturity, fear of sexuality and intimacy (Bemis, 1978), or the woman's movement creating increased performance demands, while traditional standards of attractiveness still prevail (Selvini Palazzoli, 1974).

The etiology of anorexia nervosa is not well understood (Marazzi, 1982). Studies are retrospective in nature and, for the most part, poorly controlled. Research findings are not definitive, for instance,

> There is no one family constellation nor a single type of mother-child relationship that will regularly be associated with anorexia nervosa. Rather, there are a variety of difficulties in families that may predispose to anorexia nervosa. (Garfinkel and Garner, 1982, p. 177)

Besides family-related variables, a variety of other factors have been suggested that predispose, initiate and/or maintain the disorder.

Predisposing factors may be at the individual level (identity/autonomy problems, inability to differentiate internal states, egocentrism/immature cognitive development, perceptual disturbances, weight pathology, personality structure-dependency, etc.); the familial level (history of affective illness, older parents, alcoholic fathers, exaggerated parental demands); or the cultural level (e.g., dieting as "good" behavior).

Initiating factors cited include separation and loss, new performance demands or physical illness.

Maintaining factors include family balance (maintaining the child's problem to avoid marital problems, covert coalitions, conflictual communications); physical factors (level of starvation attained, altered sense of satiation, presence of vomiting); psychological factors (disturbed body image, self-reinforcement by avoiding what is feared, unresolved conflicts); or cultural factors (emphasis on thinness) (Bruch, 1977; Minuchin et al., 1978; Garfinkel and Garner, 1982).

Anorexia nervosa has proven difficult to treat. No one treatment has been experimentally verified as effective. Behavior therapies may achieve short-term success, but not long-term adjustment (Bemis, 1978). While successful in inducing weight gain, they may have negative long-range effects by robbing patients of control—which they already severely lack (Bruch, 1977). Other suggested therapies have included such unlikely methods as ECT, insulin, antipsychotic medication (chlorpromazine), and surgery.

For most cases, a comprehensive course of treatment is necessary, recommended to include, first, hospital treatment for eight to twelve weeks to break the cycle of weight loss and curtail starvation so that the patient's weight is slowly restored up to a target weight. This is followed by continued hospitalization for about three weeks to ensure that weight restoration is maintained and to reestablish normal eating behaviors, including overcoming pain at mealtime and guilt. Finally, long-term psychotherapy should begin during hospitalization and continue after discharge, with goals of: appropriate affective expression; accurate body image perception; improved sense of self-concept and personal trust; overcoming fear of separation and feelings of emptiness and despair; and developing greater autonomy and an independent identity (Garfinkel and Garner, 1982; Bruch, 1977).

Family therapy is a desirable mode and should be the primary method for those 16 and under and living at home. Use of medications is only rarely indicated and should *never* be the sole treatment method. Assertiveness training and mutual help groups are useful adjuncts to therapy. Unless life is imminently threatened, all aspects of treatment should optimally be voluntary and part of a plan agreed upon by the patient and her family. Therapy should be avoided which takes away the patient's control or reinforces responses elicited solely to please others (rather than eliciting true feelings).

The prognosis for anorexia nervosa varies markedly, depending on patient characteristics. Death has been reported in from 0 to 24% of patients on follow-up. Outcome is usually better with pediatric cases. Overall, studies show that 40% are recovered, 30% improved, 20% remain impaired and 9% die. The duration of the illness also varies considerably, with recurrences reported three to 14 years post-recovery, usually precipitated by a stressful event such as pregnancy. Symptomatology in those with continued problems includes depression, anxiety, obsessions and social phobias (often agoraphobia).

Recently bulimia, a form of anorexia nervosa, has come to the public's attention, because of epidemic proportions of afflicted women. In bulimia, the behavior consists of bingeing then voluntarily purging, taking large quantities of laxatives, diuretics or enemas, or fasting. The binge episode consists of eating large quantities, usually junk food, high in carbohydrates, often as much as 4,000 to 5,000 calories per day or from 1,000 to 20,000 calories per binge (Corsp, 1980; Boskind-White and White, 1983). In one survey of 300 bulimics, 82% binged at least three times a week, vomiting from once weekly to 18 times per day (Boskind-White and White, 1983).

The condition is particularly prevalent in girls of high school and college age, particularly among those oriented toward academic achievement and a traditional life-style (Boskind-White and White, 1983). Solitary bulimics often go unnoticed for years, because, unlike anorexics, their weight stays within normal limits and they appear healthy. For others, bulimia is shared socially, e.g., girls who are ''barf buddies'' stuff themselves with food and then go to the bathroom together to vomit.

The consequences of bulimia may be extremely dangerous to physical health as the process of over-eating and vomiting results in the loss of many essential nutrients (e.g., potassium). Bulimia can produce hypoglycemia, gastrointestinal problems, decreased metabolism leading to depression, severe tooth decay, perpetual sore throat, inflammation of the esophagus, hiatal hernias, and swelling of the salivary glands. Extreme losses of potassium can damage heart and kidney functioning. Heavy use of laxatives and diuretics can produce dehydration, rectal bleeding, amenorrhea, or even death. Self-induced vomiting can cause reverse peristalsis or spontaneous regurgitation of the stomach contents. The extent of bulimia is unknown, with estimates ranging from 5 to 20% of all young women engaging in some form of bingeing and purging (Mayer and Goldberg, 1982). Within the bulimic population, 87% are female (Halmi et al., 1981). In relationship to anorexia nervosa, bulimia probably occurs in about 30% of these patients at some time in their illness (Corsp, 1980).

There appear to be significant differences between anorexics and bulimics. Bulimics never reach as low a weight; have a history of obesity; exhibit impulsive, self-destructive behaviors; are sexually active but without enjoyment; show more psychopathology and are likely to experience a more chronic type of illness (Garfinkel and Garner, 1982).

Another source contends that bulimics are suggestible women, more workable in therapy, more socially competent, and more in control (Boskind-White and White, 1983). Currently, the distinction between bulimia and the restricting form of anorexia is only descriptive, based on behavior. However, it is known that vomiting is a poor prognostic sign in anorexia and may be related to the duration of the disorder.

Boskind-White and White (1983) have recently labelled this syndrome "bulimarexia" to differentiate it from anorexia. They believe bulimarexia is learned behavior—maladaptive responses to a female socialization that has overemphasized the ideal. According to the Whites, bulimarexic women are characterized by strife-ridden relationships with their mothers and paternal rejection amidst secret yearnings for intimacy. They experience a lifelong quest for male approval "above all else and give men the power to define how they should act, think and feel" (p. 127).

After seven years of applied research and treatment of more than 2,000 women, the Whites have established a group therapy program to help clients unlearn this behavior. The emphasis is to increase the commitment to change and develop effective strategies to cope with stress to overcome bulimarexia. Group members begin by finding common goals in their binge/purge behaviors and identifying with each other. Each member then establishes her own goals, expectations and specific action alternatives and makes a commitment to the group. Group work focuses on establishing feelings of sisterhood, facilitating open communication, dispelling myths of perfectionism and the "bionic woman" concept, exploring sexuality and the self-loathing of their own bodies, generating alternatives, and assertiveness training. Participants are taught new strategies, like rewarding themselves for success rather than focusing on failures, talking themselves *out* of old behavior patterns, and behavior rehearsal for stressful situations. Because of the severe health problems often associated with bulimarexia, the Whites caution that any form of psychological intervention should be accompanied by medical referral and involvement.

Awareness of this disorder has been increased by actress

Jane Fonda's self-confessed bulimia. While the treatment approach described by the Whites appears promising, like other forms of anorexia, knowledge of treatment approaches proven effective remains very limited.

Case Study:
Anorexia Nervosa:
A Girl and Her Father

Elliot D. Luby
Morris Weiss

Sharon was a petite young (19-year-old) woman with an acne-scarred face and a body showing recent weight loss when she entered the hospital. She was outgoing, expressive and warm. She related easily and seemed to be strongly motivated for treatment. She possessed a full range, depth, and subtlety of feeling not often seen in anorexic women. Her mood was moderately depressed. There were themes of sadness and frustration related to her current weight loss dilemma. Her thought content revolved around issues of her fear of eating and her pathological involvement with her family.

Sharon began to avoid high-calorie foods as a college student in September of 1981. At that time, her sister was pregnant and she was revolted by her sister's appearance. She reduced her caloric intake to 100 to 500 calories per day, and she gradually began to lose weight. She felt that she was "chubby" and was not comfortable weighing over 100 pounds. She then developed a classic anorexic pattern of hyperactivity and food refusal associated with an intense food preoccupation. In March of 1982, her sister delivered. Then Sharon began to diet even more relentlessly and her weight fell to close to 90 pounds. She was seen in psychotherapy by a psychiatrist who recognized her depression and placed her on tricyclic antidepressant medicine. She felt that somehow her weight loss was tied to a compelling perfectionistic need on her part which she related to her father's excessive demands for academic achievement and success in athletics. She recalled wanting to be slim like her brothers

Drs. Luby and Weiss are psychiatrists on the Harper-Grace Hospital staff, Detroit, Michigan, and in private practice.

when she was a child in order to obtain her father's approval. By May, she was eating only 300 to 400 calories per day and her weight loss was becoming increasingly apparent. Attempts to have her agree upon a diet of at least 1,200 calories daily were unsuccessful.

As her anorexia progressed, she became clinically *less* depressed. In fact, she stated that she could only be happy if she adhered to her rigid self-imposed diet and, conversely, she became guilty and unhappy when she overate. In June, she was told by her therapist that her anorexia might interfere with her plans to attend a small private college in the fall. She began to understand that her preoccupation with food was disrupting her social contacts as well as more intimate relationships with the opposite sex. Part of her felt she was too fat and should not eat, while the other part realized that she was deteriorating physically and she should eat normally. Finally, in a statement of her despair, she took an overdose of the antidepressant medicine and was hospitalized.

The concern about her sister's pregnancy had developed because of a two-year relationship with her brother-in-law. Sharon was a passive partner in a sexual relationship which the brother-in-law controlled and maintained. She could never bring this to the attention of her parents and she could not refuse him. She believed that her sister was also an active participant in knowing about and encouraging the seduction. While she was horrified by her brother-in-law's approaches, she could do nothing about it. Finally, she did tell her parents but did not feel they reacted with appropriate anger and outrage.

Sharon was the youngest of five children. Her father was a physician and her mother was a housewife who can only be described as extremely controlling. She was the mediator or transmitter of all family communications—in a sense, a kind of central relay station. Sharon's father rarely, if ever, exhibited any positive feeling toward Sharon and there was little interaction between them. Her mother always interceded because she thought she had to protect Sharon from his hostility and rejection. The family was also characterized by a need to appear harmonious and tranquil. There was great emphasis on achievement and on a "successful and closely knit family." Prior to her coming to the hospital, her father said her disease was a "bunch of crap."

Sharon was always an excellent student. Grades were extremely important to her. She succeeded academically in high school and she then went on to college where she obtained a 4.0 average. However, as the anorexia grew in intensity she found that she was unable to study and she dropped out of school.

When Sharon entered the hospital, she was evaluted by internists who found no significant physical disease. There were changes in various blood chemistries as a result of her self-starvation. No consideration was given to feeding her intravenously or by intubation. Therefore, she was placced on a regular 2,000-calorie diet in our anorexia program where she was seen in individual psychotherapy, attended the anorexia group, and participated in several family sessions with her parents. The social worker observed the family dynamics as "triangulation and enmeshment with failure of individuation on Sharon's part." She was very close to her highly controlling and intrusive mother and had virtually no relationship with her uninvolved, preoccupied, and somewhat hostile father. In individual psychotherapy, the focus was on the two-year sexual relationship with the brother-in-law and on the significance of her anorexia beginning at a time when her sister became pregnant. The anorexia was seen as a rejection of that pregnancy and as a way of managing her intense fear of sexuality and adult responsibility. Over time, the rage toward her brother-in-law was increasingly expressed. The parents actively participated in the family meetings and the mother began to reduce the intrusive and controlling behavior which had characterized her over such a long period of time. Sharon spoke openly and directly to her father and complained bitterly to him about his failure to show affection or even to express any interest in what she was doing. In a highly emotional meeting, he admitted to Sharon that he had been a failure as a father and intended to change his cold and aloof behavior. During this hospitalization, the father grew closer to her while the mother gradually began the painful process of distancing herself in order to allow Sharon to separate.

After four weeks of treatment, Sharon had not only gained 15 pounds but also considerable insight into what motivated her anorexic behavior. She was discharged on a regular diet, placed on a small dose of tricyclic antidepressant drug and resumed outpatient psychotherapy. She seemed less concerned about her body weight and felt more positively about herself. She emphasized how important family therapy in the hospital was in changing her relationship with her father and described how much more communicative her parents were and how her father had become increasingly affectionate, direct and open with her. She was placed in a group for anorexic/bulimic women in which she felt strongly supported. Toward the end of the summer, she made final plans to enter a small private college in the midwest and to resume her therapy there.

It is of interest that in the ensuing two years, Sharon has won several academic prizes. She wrote a paper on rape in primitive African tribes which won a national award. She continued in outpatient psychotherapy in a special anorexia program at school, developed because of the large number of young women displaying this behavior.

Example: Agoraphobia

Agoraphobia literally translated means "fear of the marketplace," and in general usage denotes a "fear of open spaces." However, this definition only partially describes the agoraphobic's fears. The fearful situation usually involves crowds, confinement, or being away from home. Specific instances may revolve around bridges, tunnels, public transportation, elevators, stores, theaters, etc. (Mathews et al., 1981). The underlying theme behind this wide array of phobias is anxiety in situations where escape to safe territory might be hindered—the more confining the situation, the greater the amount of anxiety. Unlike other social phobias, the great majority of agoraphobics are women (60-80%). In fact, more than a million American women find themselves confined and restricted by this syndrome (Brodsky and Hare-Mustin, 1980). Most of these women are married, so agoraphobia has often been labeled the "housewives' disease" (Marks, 1970). Agoraphobia usually begins between the ages of 18 and 35, but may persist untreated for some time, so patients seen in treatment may be older (Mathews et al., 1981).

The symptoms of agoraphobia are fluctuating in severity. Their inconsistency of onset has caused great puzzlement for those trying to treat the syndrome. Agoraphobics suffer from certain symptoms not usually found in other phobic disturbances, such as high levels of chronic anxiety, depression, depersonalization and panic attacks (Marks, 1970). Physical symptoms usually include sweating, dry mouth, heart pounding and fainting. Substance abuse may further complicate the life of the agoraphobic. The pattern of onset may begin with a period of generalized anxiety that is, in part, a stress reaction. The most frequent stressor is marital dissatisfaction, but other stressors can include bereavement, physical illness, childbirth, moving to a strange setting, or sexual attack (Goldstein, 1973). The anxiety is usually relieved by the presence of a trusted companion.

An important aspect of agoraphobia is fear of fear—fears increasingly generalize to more and more situations and, because agoraphobics tend to avoid the situations that cause their distressing symptoms, their lives become more and more restricted. In this way, agoraphobia is a "hidden" condition; its prevalence may be far underestimated because oftentimes the agoraphobic lives in such seclusion that he/she is unnoticed. Because the traditional female role is tied to house and home, women agoraphobics may go unnoticed even more so than men.

The anticipation of anxiety and the accompanying symptoms:

> . . . often make the patient fear that he/she will lose control and behave in a disinhibited way, or even become insane; while rapid heart action may lead the patient to expect a cardiac arrest . . . that they may faint . . . and find themselves surrounded by unsympathetic onlookers. (Mathews et al., p. 5)

Hormonal explanations linking agoraphobia to estrogen disorders have been suggested, e.g., the fluctuating estrogen levels seen in post-partum depression and menstrual tension are similar to the patterns of onset found in some agoraphobic women; or women's low levels of testosterone may reduce aggressive, dominant behavior and thus contribute to the passive, avoidant behavior of this syndrome (Money and Erhardt, 1972). A sex role explanation has also been offered: women, not having been socialized to become self-assertive and independent, are more helpless in stressful situations and less likely to evaluate options of escape (Fodor, 1974). The anxiety associated with venturing outside the home may be part of female socialization (Hare-Mustin, 1983). While it is generally agreed that agoraphobia may be viewed as a stress syndrome, the agoraphobic generates an entire life-style based on her phobic avoidance of venturing outside.

The psychodynamics of agoraphobia have been seen as an adult version of infant separation anxiety. The agora-

phobic may be excessively dependent on a trusted attachment figure, remaining in an unhappy relationship rather
than facing a terrifying separation. Thus, a woman may be
unhappily married, but is "prevented" from leaving by her
debilitating fear. Or sometimes the feared object is a symbol
for a deeper fear, e.g., sexual encounters, death wishes toward parent or spouse, etc. Relapses in agoraphobia often
relate to deterioration in the relationship with the husband
or reappearance of marital conflicts as the agoraphobic improves (Hare-Mustin, 1983). In a larger societal context,
the agoraphobic woman fits into the sex-appropriate female
stereotype of fearfulness and dependency.

A recent summary of research and theory on agoraphobia
concludes that there is no evidence of direct inheritance and
that family factors (like instability, overprotection or lack of
parental care) are, at most, predisposing not causal influences. The histories of agoraphobics and anxiety neurotics
are really not distinguishable. The critical factor hypothesized for agoraphobia is the occurrence of an acute anxiety
episode or panic attack while out-of-doors. This experience,
combined with an early-learned pattern of avoidance, dependence on others (rather than self-reliance and active
coping), and a tendency to attribute anxiety to external pro-
voking stimuli (the physical setting) rather than to internal
conditions (stress), produce and maintain the "agoraphobic
syndrome" (Mathews et al., 1981).

In reviewing current treatment approaches, antidepressant or anxiolytic drug use alone seems to be *palliative,* not
a cure, and may worsen problems by creating further dependency and substance abuse. Benzodiazepams (e.g., valium)
seem to have declining effectiveness after four months. A
more comprehensive treatment approach should combine
anxiety reduction with the client actively practicing and
confronting the actual situations that he/she has avoided
and doing so outside of the therapy session.

There is some suggestion that self-help groups for agoraphobics may be useful, as well as family involvement, particularly in providing an alternative to overdependence on
the therapist. Group therapy has also been found to have
marked advantages, perhaps for the same reasons. Research indicates that when a therapy relationship is ter-

minated, agoraphobics may often regress, or at least fail to continue making progress.

Mathews et al. (1981) have developed a self-help intervention called "Programmed Practice" which has demonstrated effectiveness and efficiency but only in limited research studies. The main points of this intervention are: 1) the client, rather than the therapist, is responsible for running the program; 2) a suitable person is recruited to help the client; 3) the client and partner are provided simple manuals which explain graded exposure and how to cope with anxiety without reliance on tranquilizers; and 4) the therapist is an advisor, not an active helper, and limits his/her time to about five visits over a month. The overall purpose is to teach clients and their partners how to deal with agoraphobia through a minimum of professional help, using a behavioral treatment approach, with the eventual aim of discontinuing medication entirely. Contrary to some allegations concerning behavioral interventions, symptom substitution is no more likely to occur with this approach than with any other. However, although these authors assert that their treatment is beneficial, they admit having only a rudimentary understanding of how it works. Although agoraphobia can have crippling effects on a woman's entire life, not enough is known about its etiology or successful treatment.

Case Study: Agoraphobia

Robert Pohl

THE CASE

Roberta's story is fairly typical of a woman with agoraphobia. It illustrates the severity of the disorder, and the ease with which it can usually be treated.

Roberta described herself as someone who never experienced any problems during childhood. She came from a middle-class family and had no problems in school. Roberta first began to experience a great deal of difficulty in her early twenties. Although Roberta's life was in most respects going well, she began to feel nervous. She developed an "unreal feeling," and became too anxious to shop alone, travel by herself, or even stand in a grocery store line. She was afraid that she would become nervous while alone and without help, and that she would fall apart if "trapped" in a long line. The thought of traveling the expressway, where she could not easily "get out" should something go wrong, terrified her. These fears started simply as a reluctance to shop or drive, but soon became so severe that she could not even travel a few blocks unaccompanied, and just leaving the house produced considerable anxiety. She could not work or go to school.

At this point, Roberta had typical symptoms for agoraphobia. However, she was unaware of this. She knew that something was wrong, but her visits to a number of physicians led nowhere. They would examine her, find nothing, and tell her that her symptoms were not real. Roberta found the dismissal of her disabling symptoms perplexing and irritating.

Roberta finally saw a psychiatrist when she was 25-years-old.

Dr. Pohl is a psychiatrist and Chief of the Outpatient Department at Lafayette Clinic, Detroit, Michigan, where he does anxiety disorder research. He is also in private practice.

95

Her agoraphobic symptoms were obvious. Moreover, careful questioning revealed that Roberta, like almost all agoraphobics, had discrete panic (anxiety) attacks that antedated her phobic symptoms. The panic attacks consisted of a surge of anxiety, a "panicky feeling," that could occur any time, even while Roberta was home. During the attack, she would feel that she was going out of her mind and would want to return to a more secure place if away from home. She felt unreal and complained that the world looked "different." Her heart would pound, making her believe that she might die. During the attack, she would also sweat and feel short of breath; tingling sensations and a flushed feeling were common. Usually, attacks would subside in 15 to 20 minutes, although some lasted longer. After an attack was over, she was left feeling shaken and more fearful than before. These attacks occurred at least two to three times weekly.

THE TREATMENT

There are two widely accepted treatment approaches to agoraphobia with panic attacks. One approach is treatment with an antidepressant. The term "antidepressant" is really a misnomer; although these drugs were first discovered as an effective treatment for depression, it was subsequently discovered that they are useful for other disorders as well. Antidepressants prevent panic attacks from occurring in the majority of patients. Although antidepressants do not directly help phobic symptoms, they do have an indirect benefit. Panic attacks are usually the cause of agoraphobic symptoms, and once the attacks stop, phobic symptoms tend to improve over time.

The other accepted treatment approach to agoraphobia is behavior therapy. The essential feature of this treatment is to get the patient to do exactly what he or she is afraid of doing, over and over again, until the patient is no longer anxious. Usually this is done in a carefully graded fashion, moving from relatively easy situations to more difficult ones. Behavior therapy treats the phobic symptoms. However, most patients continue having panic attacks, requiring a constant effort to maintain the gains made with behavior therapy.

Fortunately, drug treatment of panic attacks and behavior treatment of phobias are complimentary approaches, and not mutually exclusive. A common strategy is to first treat the panic attacks, then to treat the phobias. Behavior therapy is more effective in the absence of panic attacks; indeed, some patients improve on their own without formal behavior therapy.

Roberta started treatment by taking the antidepressant imipramine. She was also encouraged to drive as far as possible daily and taught relaxation exercises. During the course of six weeks, imipramine was increased to a moderately high dose and the panic attacks stopped. Given her past traumatic experiences, Roberta was still afraid to travel but this fear disappeared almost completely during the following two months, with the help of daily travel exercises. Roberta was no longer disabled. Subsequently, Roberta graduated from college and went into law enforcement. She was able to drive any distance without difficulty.

The marked difference between panic anxiety and normal anxiety was demonstrated to Roberta herself by a work-related incident. While off-duty, Roberta walked into an armed robbery. She pulled out her gun, yelled "police" and a gunfight ensued. A few days later, Roberta called her psychiatrist to complain of anxiety symptoms. She startled easily, felt nervous, and had difficulty falling asleep. However, she did not feel that she was having panic attacks and she had none of the physical symptoms of panic attacks. She was reassured that these anxiety symptoms were normal, given the circumstances, and the symptoms disappeared over a few weeks.

EPILOGUE

For seven years after her initial treatment, Roberta continues to do well as long as she stays on imipramine. Whenever imipramine is discontinued, the panics recur.

This prolonged treatment for a panic disorder is common; the natural history of the disorder is often chronic and the medication, while an effective treatment, is not a cure. Roberta did stop the medication to become pregnant. During pregnancy, she remained symptom-free (a common occurrence), but four months post-partum, panic attacks returned, requiring treatment.

Panic disorders often run in families. Roberta has two sisters with the disorder; and both has also responded well to imipramine. Her mother, an alcoholic, is believed to also have panic attacks and abuses alcohol as a sort of self-treatment.

Example: Hysteria

> Hysterical personalities or characters conform more closely to normal feminine patterns of needing to be attractive, to be noticed and to be loved, than to the masculine patterns of aggression, initiative and relative independence. It is for this reason that we find hysterical distortions of personality or character much more frequently among women than among men. (Cameron, 1963)

The label "hysteria" is one of the oldest, most confusing, and most debated in terms of its usefulness in describing behavior. In psychiatric literature, the term "hysterical" generally means a configuration characterized by its feminine nature. The Cameron definition is an excellent example of sexism in diagnosis. If psychopathology is described in terms of feminine characteristics, then it is no surprise that a disorder is found to be prevalent in women. So, the only way to escape labeling is *not* to have sex-role appropriate behaviors; however, sex-role deviance can often produce labeling of its own, e.g., schizophrenia. At the very least, any female might be diagnosed as hysterical since the definition encompasses traditional female traits. This is all an exercise in circular reasoning in its most defeating aspects.

Hysterics show a female predominance ranging between two and four to one (Brodsky and Hare-Mustin, 1980). There are various explanations offered for this which range from the "absurd to plausible but not proven." The explanation offered by Plato was that women who suffer from hysteria are possessed with a disturbed, wandering uterus. Deprivation of sexual relations or being barren led to the uterus drying up, losing weight, and consequently, roaming the body in search of moisture, thus causing various manifestations of pain and disease through pressure on other organs. In the Middle Ages, much behavior we now label hysteria was called witchcraft and attributed to demonic possession. Charcot, an early French physician, attributed the condition to an organic brain defect, while Freud's explanations lay in symbolism and psychological conflicts, specifically, the absence of a penis. Post-Freudian analysts added to this the existence of oral injuries and fixations; in all cases, weakness associated with the female gender was identified as the base cause (Chodoff, 1982). The problem with symbolic interpretations is that "motives, like meanings, can always be supposed and can never be disproved" (Slater, 1982, p. 37).

Hysteria actually has several distinguishable aspects. The "hysterical personality" is characterized by emotionality, attention-seeking, superficial seductiveness, dependency, helplessness, self-dramatization, a chameleon-like personality, self-indulgence, sexual problems, and a cognitive style that is diffuse, imprecise and exaggerated (Chodoff, 1982; Mackinnon and Michels, 1971). On the other hand, the hysterical conversion reaction (HCR) refers to somatic problems which appear to have no organic basis but are rather a transformation of psychic stresses into symptoms which produce primary and secondary gain (Weintraub, 1983). Some interrelate these two aspects through the assertion that the hysterical personality is an outgrowth or cause of conversion reactions. However, in other literature, hysterical personalities may exist independently.

Epidemic or mass hysteria is another use of the concept, describing outbreaks of illness involving a large number of individuals, but having no identified causes or physical findings. Schools and work environments are typical settings. Often, children or adolescents are the victims. The extent to which hysteria is associated with femininity is exemplified in mass hysteria also: one criteria for applying this diagnosis is that females make up 70% to 100% of those afflicted (Weintraub, 1983).

The hysterical personality or syndrome (with HCR) is undoubtedly the most diffuse and sexist aspect of hysteria. In recognition of this, some clinicians have abandoned or discredited it, focusing only on the conversion reaction or separating out the latter by renaming it Briquet's-Syndrome.

DSM III has omitted any reference to personality type as part of HCR. The extent to which HCR by itself represents diagnostic sexism, however, is still questionable. HCR is vastly over-represented in women, reportedly only one in a thousand cases are male (Weintraub, 1983).

Seiden (1976) contends that vaguely-defined body complaints are more likely to be diagnosed as "hysteria" in women, whereas similar symptoms in men tend to be diagnosed as "hypochondriasis" and that in physical examinations the complaints of men are taken more seriously.

Weintraub (1983) presents a seemingly objective diagnosis for HCR, indicating that there must be *positive* evidence that the distinction is *not* organic, e.g., through the presence of inconsistencies on examination and/or symptom change through suggestion. He presents several concrete tests to identify these inconsistencies, e.g., where the sensory loss reported is physiologically impossible. For cases of HCR in sensory and motor areas, the problem is usually specific (paralysis, blindness, etc.) and the diagnosis often appears clear-cut. However, unfortunately, the most common applications of HCR diagnosis *and* the most difficult involve cases of chronic pain. These complaints are continuous and do not respond to any medical or pharmacological treatments. Gynecological problems are especially frequent. The high incidence of this type of complaint may lead one to wonder how many of these HCR cases are the result of the physician blaming the patient (by labeling her a hysteric) because of *his* inability to successfully identify and diagnose her treatment or are the results of the dearth of medical research on female physiology.

> Men have little instinctive aptitude or empathy with women; and they are in any case liable to write off specifically feminine ways of thinking, feeling and acting as 'hysterical.' Faced by symptoms they do not understand, in women who do not engage their sympathy, the male doctors find an easy way out in relegating them to a category, to a diagnosis, 'hysteria,' which follows these hapless patients from one centre to another and becomes a self-fulfilling prophecy. (Slater, 1982, p. 39)

Reports from the literature indicate that anywhere from 61% to 87% of persons originally diagnosed as HCR are found to have specific organic disease or a prominent affective disorder, rather than hysterical symptoms (Kendell, 1982).

The most common explanation for hysterical conversion reactions is that because of sexual, developmental and/or environmental stress and feelings of helplessness and frustration, a subconscious alteration of the sensory and/or motor system occurs (Engel, 1970). The symptoms or dysfunction produced provide a defense against extreme anxiety, stress or psychic conflict. The area afflicted may relate to symbolic or functional reasons or knowledge of a particular illness. In any event, there is usually primary (reduction stress) as well as secondary gain (sympathy) involved. HCR may be explained in psychodynamic terms (converting repressed anxiety into the bodily symptom) or in learning and role theory (the sick role as an escape from life demands or specific circumstances that are overwhelming).

In some reported cases, usually *specific* sensory/motor losses, once the psychic basis of the problem is revealed to the patient, and counseling provided, the symptom disappears. Appropriate methods for revealing this might include suggestion, placebo, sodium amytal or hypnosis (Weintraub, 1983). In other cases, mostly involving chronic pain or multiple symptoms, problems may continue for years, unchanged by medical or psychiatric interventions. Kendell (1982) suggests long-term therapy which ignores the symptoms, avoids discussing their cause and instead focuses on minimizing the advantages of sickness. Work with the patient's family should be included in this approach.

One of the more plausible current explanations for the prevalence of HCR is that the ''sick'' role is more acceptable for women in our culture. The conversion illness often makes it difficult or impossible for a woman to carry out her familial responsibilities while simultaneously making her dependent on her family. These behaviors may be more tolerable in women and cause less conflict than an overt rejection of domestic responsibility. Or, the sick role may represent manipulative behaviors to achieve power not legitimately available. Another approach explains the disorder as a caricature of femininity:

> The displays of hysterical women represent an exaggeration of normal behavior under cultural pressure . . . a very important, causative factor is the dominating and belittling expectations of men toward women. (Chodoff, 1982, p. 549)

Hysteria may be seen as an extreme way of coping for those women who have accepted traditional feminine qualities as desirable and attempt to deal with their problems by exaggerating these ways of behaving.

In summary, problems labeled as hysterical conversion reactions of an acute or chronic nature are significant (reportedly involving 5 to 50% of cases in the physician's office, Weintraub, 1983); and 1 to 2% of the female population, (Woodruff et al., 1982); and can have extreme effects on a woman's ability to function. There is still considerable reason to question the accuracy of such labeling, either as a reflection of diagnostic sexism or as a lack of accurate knowledge of female physiology. On the other hand, there is undoubtedly some reality to the existence of HCR and its prevalence in women, which reflects the dependent role women are expected to play in our culture and the fact that a woman's direct assertion of complaints or refusal to be at the service of others is less acceptable than playing the sick role. This is well summarized by Chodoff (1982):

> Women suffer these afflictions or behave in this fashion not because of anything inherent in their nature. Rather, they are prone to hysteria because of cultural and environmental forces . . . [that] men have produced, or rather have invented, the myth of a unique femininity. (p. 546)

Whatever one's understanding of the psychodynamics of hysterical conversion reactions, it is generally agreed that this diagnosis carries the most potential for sexist bias and interpretation. The prevalence of hysterical conversion reactions during wartime shows that this response-type may be within us all. Effective treatment of HCR cannot be expected until diagnostic accuracy and medical management improve. Applying the label of hysteria, with its negative personality characteristics and implications of malingering, may *create* disturbance in and of itself.

Case Study:
Hysteria

Susan Lanir

Marge was 40-years-old, divorced and a mother of two girls ages 11 and 13. She was referred to me by the head psychiatrist in the institute where I worked at the time. Her major presenting problem was uncontrollable and painful cramping in her left hand.

At our first meeting, Marge appeared nervous and restless. I asked her about her agitation and she explained that at the recent intake interview with the psychiatrist she had "freaked" when she saw the word H-Y-S-T-E-R-I-C-A-L written in capital letters across her file. Since then, she had felt very depressed and anxious about "that word." She began to ask me about its meaning. Did it mean she was crazy? Was she out of control? Was she "nutty?" Her final comment was "I hate hysterical women."

During our early sessions, we probed the past and found out that Marge's symptom appeared for the first time three years ago. Her early childhood was very painful. She was born in England during World War II and had been sent to an orphanage in infancy so she would not be endangered by the bombing. At the end of the war her mother did not bring her home, explaining that her father had been killed in the war and she was unable to support her. Life continued at the orphanage until the age of 16 when Marge left, got a job as a secretary and saved enough money to leave the country. Before leaving, she confronted her mother about her past while asking for some financial help. Her mother, in a burst of anger, told her that her father was not dead; in fact, Marge was illegitimate and she did not know who the father was.

Susan Lanir, after the birth of her first child, gave up a career of teaching in despair, in spite of the adamant advice of her mother that "you'll be home when you have children." After a mid-life change, she is now pursuing a career in social work, lecturing on women's mental health issues and maintaining a private clinical practice.

This information led to a mild depression, expressed through feelings of helplessness and worthlessness. Once in the U.S., Marge married immediately to a salesman of South American origin. The marriage was not happy. The couple was unable to communicate with each other and found no intimacy. Instead, they substituted a life in the "swinging" world, despite the birth of two daughters. A few years after the birth of the second daughter, the couple divorced, leaving Marge with custody of both children. At this point, life became an intense financial struggle.

Marge's major pastimes were swimming and handiwork. She functioned as a secretary and mother, but felt depressed most of the time. There were frequent suicidal thoughts, but concern for her daughters repressed these and provided motivation for continuing to function.

Marge's therapy centered on working through her feelings of anger, rage and early pain around rejection. In therapy, Marge and I made a contract to ignore the hand symptom and work on getting to know herself and her feelings. However, each session always contained an anxious question about "my hysteria." I told her that I was never comfortable with that type of diagnosis and felt that it didn't really explain what was happening with her hand, but this didn't appear to satisfy her.

As the therapy progressed, she began to feel better about herself, but the hand symptom did not disappear. Seven sessions later, Marge and I were discussing pain and what that meant for her in her life. In a very off-hand way, she mentioned that four and one-half years ago there had been an accident at work and her left hand had been mangled in a machine. Two minor operations were needed. After the surgery, the hand had functioned more or less normally until three years ago when the symptom began.

I asked her if she had told the neurologist about the accident. She said yes, but he had still found nothing wrong. The psychiatrist in the intake had not asked her about any previous physical history. In our first interview I had asked her about any previous physical history, but she had not mentioned the surgery or the accident. At this point, I recommended that Marge see another neurologist and be fully open about the accident. The second neurologist also found nothing wrong but sent her to intensive physiotherapy. Within six months of physiotherapy, the hand symptom disappeared.

Despite Marge's lack of openness about her hand, my skepticism about hysterical diagnosis seemed vindicated. Both the first neurologist and the psychiatrist had been very quick to label the hand symptom as "hysterical" or "psychoneurotic." It was assumed that Marge's background "justified" "hysterical" cramping of the hand. However, the ephemeral and inappropriate nature of the diagnosis itself caused Marge great and unnecessary anxiety. Yes, Marge had—and has—her problems. She is still in need of further therapy, but an "hysterical" cramping hand, thanks to the physiotherapist, is no longer one of those problems.

Summary and Recommendations: Eliminating Sexist Treatment

I finally figured it out. You weren't supposed to be angry. Oh no. They lock you up, throw away the key, and you're supposed to smile at them, compliment the nurses, shuffle baby—so that's what I did to get out.

Former Mental Health Consumer
(Rohrbaugh, 1979)

Case studies and personal accounts of women's recent experiences in the mental health system have raised many questions. For instance, practices of automatically assuming a woman would return to the marital situation without finding out whether or not that situation may be the *primary* cause of the disturbance; misdiagnoses and misprescription of psychotropic drugs whose side effects produce psychotic-like symptoms; psychiatric commitments to get rid of trouble-making wives and mothers; restrictions in inpatient and residential settings applied because women showed anger or otherwise violated stereotypical female behaviors. Many of these inappropriate practices reported to the Michigan Women's Task Force were highly similar to those reported by Chesler in her exposé best-seller, *Women and Madness,* 15 years ago or even to cases she cited from the 1800s. And while mental health clients and direct care staff presented startling information on differential treatment of females, many of the administrative and psychiatric staff, especially in inpatient facilities, expressed a total lack of awareness or even denial of the possibility that this was occurring. A recent publication has concluded, "the chronically mentally ill are regarded as almost genderless" (Test and Berlin, 1981).

Broverman (1970) noted a decade ago that the sex biases

and stereotypes of mental health professionals matched those found in society in general. There is a double standard of mental health for men and women: to be considered a "normal," mentally healthy female, a woman must be emotional, passive, and non-competitive. However, in a classic double-bind, it is only through traits which are inappropriate to the female sex role that she is seen as a mentally healthy adult. Of course, such inappropriate sex role behavior can confer a deviant and sometimes crazy label itself.

Diagnoses as well as treatments may be based on stereotypical assumptions. Numerous studies have confirmed the existence of sex differences in mental illness in terms of definition, prevalence, and service utilization (Al-Issa, 1980; Brodsky and Hare-Mustin, 1980). Women may be diagnosed as mentally ill for exhibiting certain traits that in men are considered healthy, such as expressing anger. Societal role expectations dictate that for women anger should not be felt or expressed and often when a woman openly expresses anger, she is labeled "hysterical."

Women in our society have traditionally been socialized to be "other-directed." Traditional ideals of "femininity" have been founded on certain assumptions of helplessness, to the detriment of women's sense of competency and control. The "learned helplessness" which is a part of female socialization may be responsible for women perceiving themselves as optionless in many situations, and feeling their behavior has no influence on their outcome. Such feelings of helplessness can and do lead to depression in many cases. Testimony presented at public forums alleged that besides misdiagnoses, clinicians may inappropriately deal with anger in female clients in other ways: by overmedicating to suppress anger or by recommending that discharge or movement into a less restrictive setting be delayed until anger is no longer displayed.

It should be stressed, at this point, that a biological basis for sex differences in depression or other mental health problems has *not* been substantiated. A more reasonable explanation is that they result from socialization practices, environmental influences, and differential treatment.

The American Psychological Association Task Force on Sex Bias and Sex Role Stereotyping (1975) found sexist problems in the psychotherapeutic process with women particularly concerning traditional roles and functions. Therapists' expectations that women behave in passive and dependent ways contradict the way women *need* to act in order to be mentally healthy. Many women who have been in treatment in the mental health system say that therapy is primarily oriented to producing adjustment to existing societal expectations rather than promoting and encouraging personal growth and independence. At the same time, it must be made clear that the new wave of encouraging independence may not be appropriate movement in therapy for *all* women. Many women who are content with their primary role of homemaker and mother should not be prodded into role change needlessly.

Another priority that came to the attention of the Women's Task Force was the manner in which many mental health professionals foster dependency (including subordination and submissiveness) and prolong treatment for their clients, versus encouraging individuation and growth. Although a certain amount of dependency is expected in a therapeutic relationship, therapists must be aware that their tendency to foster dependency may be especially problematic for women clients, particularly since the treatment situation is often that of male psychiatrist—female client.

A number of specific disorders have been repeatedly substantiated to have far greater prevalence in females than males. However, there is an extreme lack of knowledge as to etiology, effective treatment, estimated incidence and prevalence or even whether an actual syndrome of identifiable set of symptoms exist. The information that is available suggests that alternatives to traditional one-on-one psychotherapy may be more effective for these disorders, e.g., group therapy, behavioral approaches, etc., since the traditional approach often involves a female client and male therapist interacting in such a way as to maximize sex biases entering into the treatment. The Women's Task Force maintains that more research should be carried out, especially concerning behavioral approaches, to identify effective treatment for disorders prevalent in females, particularly agoraphobia, anorexia nervosa, and hysteria.

A greater emphasis also needs to be placed on group

work with all clients. The development of supportive relationships with other women is a crucial dimension of group work. Furthermore, by observing how other women have handled similar problems, women become more aware of options applicable to their own lives.

All too frequently in the past, mental health professionals have blamed mothers for their children's emotional difficulties rather than providing them with assistance and support. Women are the persons in a family most likely to seek help and are the ones most likely to approach mental health agencies. Knowing this, therapists need to involve fathers and families in therapy. Treating the family as a unit helps to remove much of this blame from women, or prevent women from excluding fathers in treatment. Family therapy seeks to treat the entire system rather than focus entirely on the symptomatic member.

Today clinicians should not examine a woman without understanding the system in which she moves. This is especially true for poor women. Many poor women have tremendous difficulties once they come into contact with the mental health system—especially poor women coming from different ethnic and cultural backgrounds. It is often difficult for the mental health worker to understand behavior without being familiar with the cultural nuances of the individual in treatment. If this understanding does not exist, misdiagnoses easily occur.

Other problems in treating female clients have also emerged from case studies and testimony presented to the Women's Task Force. Because of child care responsibilities and not having their own cars, female clients may often be locked into their own homes and so drop out or not be able to begin participation in center-based programs unless special arrangements are made. The needs of the long-term mentally disabled as mothers appear to be almost totally neglected (Test and Berlin, 1981), even though there are models for services that could be built upon, e.g., infant mental health and children of disordered adults interventions. There is a need also for recognition and appropriate response to the special personal hygiene needs of the female clients and the greater significance which hygiene and appearance play in social acceptance and normalization for females. Another problem involves vocational training. Because of stereotypes involving women's roles or traditional occupations, women may be referred for vocational training less frequently or for limited types of training. This reduces the availability of a significant resource in the continuum of service opportunities that should be available and consequently lowers employability and earnings. Female clients are also more likely than males to be subject to sexual harassment or victimization. The result of unwelcome sexual contact (e.g., rape, unwanted pregnancy or abortion) is also more severe and traumatizing to women. Women clients need to be afforded some protection from sexual exploitation or mistreatment, but also need to be given information and training that enables them to protect themselves, e.g., appropriate and inappropriate sexual behavior in public, birth control information, etc.

The Women's Task Force has found that professional schools have not adequately prepared their students to deal with the problems of contemporary women. They are not prepared to help them work through difficulties caused by powerlessness and alienation. Since societal changes are demanding more flexibility in sex-role performance, both women and men are finding it imperative to experience a greater diversity of roles. Human service professionals must be prepared to help both men and women adapt to these changes.

Therefore, there is a tremendous need to integrate new information on men, women and sex roles into the training and education of mental health professionals. Therapists can be in highly influential and powerful positions vis-à-vis their clients. They must be nonjudgmental and aware of biases and tendencies within themselves that result in distorted perceptions of women which may be harmful to female clients.

The Women's Task Force public forums yielded many recommendations to improve the administration of public mental health services. The Task Force stresses the need for administrators and supervisors to hire mental health counselors (both men and women) who are free of chauvinistic attitudes. The Task Force further maintains that it is crucial that supervisors and counselors pay attention to those attitudes not only in hiring, but in supervision as well. It is time for stereotypical notions about females and their roles to be eliminated from mental health evaluations and interventions. More attention needs to be given to the stress women experience living under a double standard. The elimination of sex bias and sex-role stereotyping is absolutely necessary in order for the public mental health system to truly promote mental health in women.

In addition, women must take a more prominent, assertive role on community mental health boards and in administrative positions, to accelerate the move from an outmoded, male-dominated institutional system to a more flexible, family- and community-oriented system in women.

RECOMMENDATIONS

A. Direct Services

1. In cases of females seeking mental health services for themselves or their children, there should be greater insistence on and use of family therapy to avoid placing the responsibility for the family's problems on the mother alone and to emphasize building support systems into the family as a whole to help in reduction of stress. Every effort should be made to involve the spouse and the entire family in treatment. This is particularly important for teenage mothers.

2. Issues of treatment and commitment are fundamentally human rights issues; nevertheless, sexist attitudes do exist and can further complicate successful treatment of the female client. It is recommended that helping professionals, especially psychiatrists, change attitudes toward accepting women's expression of anger as healthy, rather than pathological and that appropriate displays of anger should not be extinguished with drugs.

3. In assigning therapists for counseling, care should be taken in assigning women, particularly those with role-related problems, to counselors who are sympathetic to and have training on women's mental health problems.

4. Mental health professionals should be required to provide careful and comprehensive diagnostic ser vices to women seeking help for a serious mental health problem, including taking a medical history. Referrals for medication should only be made when necessary according to the diagnostic assessment.

5. Mental health professionals should review the need for referral to vocational training for women as well as men. Referrals for women should consider more than the traditional female occupations. Based on the client's skills and interests, training for factory work, maintenance or other male-dominated occupations might provide a more appropriate, economically rewarding and stable job in the future.

6. As part of the case management function, the mental health system should support follow-through type services for severely disabled women, such as job-finding; despite budget constraints, such services may reduce the total cost of an individual's mental health care by reducing recidivism.

7. Mental health agencies should place priority on serving women clients in group therapy. There may be greater and faster movement with women in groups than individually; women in groups benefit from seeing how their problems are related to societal roles and expectations plus by seeing other women's strengths and weaknesses. Groups may also have the advantage of taking an educational focus rather than a mental illness focus with its stigmatizing connotations. Therapists for women's groups should also be women and they should be able to become group members themselves, sharing their fears and experiences.

8. As part of the client services management function, service providers should *teach* women how to make use of support services and should advocate for their clients with other agencies and institutions. Women need direct help in getting other services, not just referrals, and they need to know what to do when they hit obstacles.

9. Treatment programs for severely disturbed women should include the opportunities for women to meet

in an informal group to explore and research their lives together in order to develop the context and meaning of their experiences as women.

10. Therapists should be encouraged to make home visits, as appropriate, particularly to low income female clients so they get a better sense of the client's situational and life problems. These are significant for the directions and content of therapy.

11. In treatment planning for severely disturbed female clients, the treatment team should consider issues of sex education and birth control. There needs to be a greater awareness particularly of the problems of women that are released from mental health facilities. Proper family planning knowledge should be provided as part of the case management function.

12. Mental health programs must be responsive to the needs of chronically mentally ill women who are mothers, by providing a range of services to increase parenting skills and to cope with the stresses of parenthood, e.g., child management skill training, access to child care, training in recognizing children's needs, and coping with personal needs vs. others' demands (Test and Berlin, 1981).

13. Inpatient facilities and residential programs should ensure females have adequate and easy access to essential personal hygiene supplies, e.g., soap, shampoo, deodorant, sanitary napkins and tampons.

14. Mental health programs, especially those for long-term mentally disabled women, should ensure that adequate assistance is given regarding hygiene and appearance, including attention to side effects of medication which detract from appearance, like acne, weight gain, etc.

B. Administration of Mental Health Services

1. Mental health agencies need to be more sensitive to the fact that women have a greater need for support services of transportation (since they have less access to cars than men) and child care (since they have this as a primary responsibility). For high risk women to

receive the necessary mental health services, these needs must be met. The public mental health system should identify the extent of these needs and make efforts to meet them. Innovative solutions to these problems should be explored such as Foster Grandparents as babysitters, ride-sharing among clients, cooperation with community bus services, etc.

2. In order to fully promote family therapy, mental health agencies must provide more flexibility in hours, such as opportunities for evening and Saturday appointments. These agencies must also ensure that ample space is provided for family sessions.

3. Because females are more likely to be sexually victimized and sexually controlled, it is of extreme importance to female clients that there be a policy on human sexuality. This policy should consider individual rights and the need for a normalized environment and be reviewed by groups of former clients.

4. The current status of sterilization laws for mentally disabled persons should be reviewed, including consent issues, to develop recommendations for public policy and statutes.

5. Mental health patients may be regarded as less than human which often results in demoralizing treatment. The mental health system should carefully examine the quality and quantity of services provided to women, e.g., extended treatment fostering dependency and perpetuating a secondary status of women in general. The treatment of females within facilities must be carefully examined for this reason.

6. Allegations of problematic areas in women's treatment should be investigated through special evaluation and research studies. It is crucial that a stronger emphasis be placed on research pertaining to women's mental health. Examples may include:

   a. the disproportionate number of women referred to dependent placements at discharge,
   b. differential and inappropriate reasons cited for females' admissions or discharges (no makeup, hair uncombed, sexual promiscuity),

   c. differences in length of treatment by program
      elements,
   d. sex differences in medication practices.
7. Attitudes and practices toward women in inpatient
   psychiatric facilities must be re-examined to determine if doctors perceive men's complaints to be more
   significant and if there is a different standard of diagnosis for females.
8. An important part of improving women's mental
   health treatment would be increasing emphasis on
   program evaluation of women's services in CMH since
   it can: produce facts to counter myths and stereotypes; identify women's actual problems so that programs can better match needs; and involve men in
   data gathering and analysis to promote consciousness-raising.
9. Inpatient mental health facilities should review discharge practices to ensure that clinicians are sensitive
   to the fact that returning females to their husbands
   may be an exacerbation of their mental health problems and a limiting of growth and development opportunities. Clinicians should specifically examine this
   question in doing discharge planning.

C. Training for Mental Health Professionals

1. The pervasiveness of sex biases in traditional therapeutic approaches should be examined by the public
   mental health system in conjunction with training and
   academic resources and professional organizations to
   change basic attitudes and therapeutic ways of relating to women, and to establish goals for changing curriculum and training practices.
2. Mental health professionals not trained by women are
   less likely to have developed skills to listen to women;
   therefore, more faculty and clinical supervisors should
   be female.
3. The professional schools should ensure that their
   students get adequate training in roles and skills other
   than traditional therapy, e.g., family therapy, group
   therapy, client services management, planning, coor-

dination, community development and skills to better manage individuals *and* systems.

4. Society is grounded in terms of male experience. Therefore, when a woman experiences madness, she experiences the double burden of the madness itself with no context for understanding. Medical and professional schools must examine their curriculum to determine the extent to which female experiences and their meanings are reflected and make necessary changes.

5. As part of their training, therapists should be made aware of the role of dependency and its reinforcement in female patients. Development of treatment plans and their review should include this as a key principle.

D. Continuing Education/Inservice Training

1. Therapists should be made aware of their sex role biases in treating women; this can best be achieved in groups, not didactically; awareness must be increased before other types of training will be effective.

2. Training of physicians in the public mental health system should include a special focus on improving their understanding of women, particularly for those from cultures which differ from those of the clients they are treating: cultural differences in the roles of women are even greater than those for men.

3. Therapists' training in appropriately serving females must include an awareness of the individual client's social/family/economic situation and the stresses which this creates and should recognize that these stresses along with social bias and discrimination may be legitimate reasons for women's anger.

4. Specific training should focus on the following: skills and sensitivity concerning women's role overload, normal developmental crises and life tasks, use of medication with women; inappropriate diagnosis, labeling and hospitalization for women because they internalize problems or do not fit traditional stereotypes; inappropriate therapeutic goals based on traditional stereotypes; aspects of normal and pathological

grief processes; recognition of how social norms can prevent women's self-actualization and the conflicts this produces; techniques to decrease stress through more democratization of housework and increasing responsibility in children.

5. Training for mental health professionals and case reviews need to address the implicit assumption that a woman's treatment should be geared to returning her to the marital situation or parental home.

6. The mental health system should form women's issues groups to help educate staff members on women's issues.

E. Public Policy Support

1. The mental health system should help publicize the importance of therapists' attitudes in treatment of female clients and make available to the public the names of persons who identify themselves as non-sexist therapists in the public and private sectors. It is also recommended that appropriate referrals to non-sexist therapists also be considered according to the client's ability to pay.

2. The public mental health system should support more research on normal and pathological development in females and females' psychological functioning and mental health problems in order to correct the fact that much of the female treatment is premised on theory and research developed solely out of the male experience.

3. There needs to be more research on the interaction between hormones, nutrition and their effects on behavior. Diets of many women may be unnecessarily contributing to problems (Tourre, 1981).

SECTION 4:
WOMEN AND THEIR PHYSICIANS:
THE EVIDENCE

MEDICATION DIFFERENCES

Sex role stereotyping and bias are strongly reflected in the medication practices of physicians. Statistics produced show alarming rates of medication for women (President's Commission on Mental Health, 1978). Of more than 229 million prescriptions for psychoactive drugs issued in 1978, 80% of amphetamines, 67% of tranquilizers and 60% of barbiturates and sedatives were prescribed for women. Twice as many women as men use the popular tranquilizers, valium and librium (Manheimer, Mellinger and Balter, 1968), while 50% more women than men report having used barbiturates for medical purposes. In a national study, 13% of women report having used psychotherapeutic prescription drugs during the past year (Parry et al., 1973). Similar findings apply to women in Canada, the U.S. and Great Britain (Cooperstock, 1976). Ninety percent of the professionals who prescribe psychoactive drugs are male (P.C.M.H. Report, 1978), e.g., general practitioners or internists, and 90% of the psychotropic drugs women use are obtained by prescription from a physician. Overall, physicians write 73% of psychotropic drug prescriptions to women and 27% to men. While women make up 58% of all doctors' visits, they receive 78% of all prescriptions for psychotropic drugs (Fidell, 1977). Physicians also report that women have 63% of the unexplained symptoms, 61% of the psychiatric symptoms, and 60% of all psycho-

121

somatic illnesses (Kravits et al., 1975). In other research, general practitioners have described a "typically complaintive patient" as a woman 72% of the time (Cooperstock, 1976). While prescriptions for minor tranquilizers have decreased markedly in recent years, the sex-ratio of 2 to 1, female to male prescriptions has been maintained (Balter, 1981). Finally, rates of over-the-counter usage tend to be the same for women and men suggesting that sex differences occur primarily in prescribed psychotropic drugs, while the tendency to self-medicate with non-prescription, mood-modifying drugs does not differ by sex (Fidell, 1977).

The basic issue is whether women are being overmedicated. There is no current research proving that these statistics present a case for over-medication, but the data raise some critical questions. Are the drugs being prescribed to those with genuine mental health problems or is a woman medicated by her male doctor because of failure of communication, based on sex stereotypes? Do the drugs facilitate solution of the patient's emotional/situational problems or might they not promote acceptance rather than problem resolution? Is misuse or abuse of drugs recognized when they are obtained from legitimate sources (e.g., from one or more physicians)?

Two-thirds of all prescription drug abusers are female and the total population of these abusers is thought to be four times that of heroin abusers (Parry, 1971). However, most drug treatment programs are focused on the heroin addict rather than the drug prescription abuser in spite of existing evidence that women request treatment for prescription drug abuse when treatment is offered (Dammann, 1977).

The use and misuse of drugs in the elderly has clearly been substantiated. Twenty-five percent of all prescription drugs sold are for people over age 65. And one out of five of these prescriptions is for psychoactive drugs (U.S. Department of Health, Education, and Welfare, 1979). In Michigan, one-fourth of older adults use four or more prescription medicines daily and it is not unusual to find a person who takes ten different medicines per week (Substance Abuse Among Michigan's Senior Citizens, 1978). In fact, in one hospital, 65% of the "emotional problems" of new admissions to the geriatric unit were related to medication usage

(Are They Worth It?, 1980). Drug-related problems in our older population is a major concern—especially when considering that the majority of this elderly population are women.

STEREOTYPIC NOTIONS

Stereotypic notions about females and their roles may influence patient evaluation and treatment method selection. For instance, in one study, 87% of physicians judged that daily use of minor tranquilizers was legitimate for housewives, but only 53% considered even occasional use as legitimate for students with even lower percentages for persons in other situations (Fidell, 1977). Depressed menopausal women may often receive hormonal therapy and/or psychotropic medication rather than counseling to deal with role loss (Bart and Grossman, 1978).

Women may be more vulnerable to stereotyped perceptions because doctor-patient dominance is compounded when the male is the prescriber/healer while the female is the passive, dependent recipient. For example, women are more ready to label themselves as psychiatrically ill, enter treatment and accept their patient role (Horowitz, 1977). Women are also more compliant about actually taking medication prescribed (Greenberg et al., 1973). It also appears that male physicians take the medical complaints of men more seriously than those of women. For instance, one study examined the response of male physicians to identical complaints of male and female clients and found that work-ups for men were significantly more extensive.

Researchers in Canada have found patterns of drug usage similar to those in the United States. One explanation offered is that sex differences in prescription rates are rooted in sex stereotypes, whereby any deviation from the role of wife, mother, sex-object and "self-sacrificing nurturer" is perceived by prescribing physicians as sick. Rather than recognizing the stresses in women's roles and helping them cope with this, physicians prescribe drugs which serve to reinforce traditional stereotypes of women's status and their other-serving nature (Stephenson and Walker, 1980).

The following case study is an example of women being prescribed psychotropic medication when facing a crisis rather than being supported and aided in developing positive coping mechanisms for going through the normal stages of the grieving process.

> Sixteen-year-old Kelly K. was referred to me because of depression, weight gain, and promiscuity. Her father had died two years previously, yet Kelly and her mother first discussed the event in my office. They described the horror of Mr. K.'s sudden death and how both of them had been told by their priest, family doctor, friends, and neighbors to put on brave faces and try to cope, "don't let your father/husband down." The family doctor accompanied his suggestions with large doses of tranquilizers for them both for the next few months. On withdrawal of the medication, both had experiences which they felt "showed I was going crazy." Kelly felt her father was still around; she could hear his voice and smell his pipe. Mrs. K. felt overwhelmed by angry feelings about her husband leaving her with the children. Neither could share these strange feelings with the other. Mrs. K. became withdrawn and preoccupied, and then worried about Kelly's defiance, overeating and staying out late "with the wrong group."
>
> Once their feelings were put into perspective as normal manifestations of the second stage of grief, the onset of which had been greatly delayed by the use of medication, mother and daughter were able to cry together, work through their feelings, and begin to accept the fact of Mr. K.'s death. (Stephenson and Walker, 1980, p. 31)

Stereotypic notions of physicians about "women's illnesses" also contribute to overmedication and misdiagnoses. Ann Wright, a counselor for Drug Help in Ann Arbor, Michigan, reported "I've had two women in the last year and a half who were given Elavil (anti-depressant) for depression. Actually, it turned out they had low blood sugar."

Depression is a common side effect of birth control pills. Ms. Wright continued,

> I've had many women come in on tranquilizers and anti-depressants who were suffering from improper hormone balances from birth control pills. It happened to me. I was on librium for two years for depression, prescribed by different doctors and University Health Service. They wanted me to see a psychiatrist, too. Finally, a female doctor there realized I had a hormone imbalance from birth control pills. After she switched my prescription, I was fine. Doctors just do not pay enough attention to depression in women caused by hormone imbalances. (Ann Wright, 1980)

Another contributant to use of psychotropic medications is that women often present themselves to physicians with primary or secondary complaints concerning their reproductive functions, e.g., dysmenorrhea, amenorrhea, postpartum depression, menopause, etc. Since these are disorders that are less well-researched and with which physicians (predominantly male) have little personal experience, an understandable tendency is for them to view what they do not understand and what they have difficulty treating as due to psychological problems (Lenane and Lenane, 1973). Consequently, they apply psychotropic drugs.

These practices may suggest societal tendencies to maintain women in a second-class status as well as to uphold stereotypes that define their roles and expected behaviors. For women, feelings of powerlessness, helplessness and dependency may be intensified through use of psychotropic drugs. These drugs place women in the sick role and conveniently ignore societal flaws that may very well be the causative factors. The treatment goal for these women is to help them ''cope,'' which in fact, equates to conformance to the stereotyped and traditional role. Psychotropic medication, it has been asserted, usually facilitates reduction in *symptomology,* rather than causative stress factors. It is used for adjustment to, rather than resolution of underlying problems. Thus, in the case of a loved one's death, for example, a woman can be sufficiently soothed and her anxiety relieved without ever completely going through the normal grieving process. Abuses may be the rule, rather than the exception, for women treated with psychotropic medication. Routine practice should be to question the effectiveness, appropriateness, and clinical suitability of treatment focused on medication alone.

Inappropriate and overuse of psychotropic medication with women is critical. It can affect a woman's ability to function in and/or outside her home and her relationships with the important people around her. Furthermore, dependency on these drugs can create a lower sense of self-esteem, feelings of powerlessness, helplessness and a fear of functioning without chemical help.

SEXIST DRUG ADVERTISING

Drug advertising, by portraying women in stereotypic roles and emotional situations, can reinforce sex biases and encourage the administration of drugs to women. In the following example, the demeaning and derogatory image of women is obvious:

> An advertisement for an anti-depressant urges "Don't settle for half-measures." The patient is a middle-aged woman, with anguished eyes, a deeply furrowed brow, and grey-brown hair swept severely back from her face. She is clothed all in black. Her face, divided in half vertically, is banded horizontally with pink and yellow on one side, and vertically with yellow and green on the other. Whether she represents the mythical repressed, frustrated and unhappy spinster, or a recent widow, the message is clear. She can only be half a woman, as she is, and needs medication. (Stephenson and Walker, 1980, p. 28)

Advertisements often portray drugs as the best treatment to help women cope with traditional roles. A journal advertisement for an anti-depressant shows a pretty young woman going down some stairs carrying a full laundry basket. The caption reads, "In depression—first get the patient moving" (Stephenson and Walker, 1980, p. 28).

The temptation to continue showing examples is overwhelming. Physicians are presented with a devalued, discounted image of female patients, while the mental health professional portrayed is hardly ever a woman (Serdenburg, 1974).

To ensure the *appropriate* use rather than misuse or abuse of psychotropic drugs with women patients will require physician education, a focus from regulatory agencies, correcting the practices of medical journals and pharmaceutical companies, and training for the patients themselves to be more assertive and question the prescribing of psychotropic drugs. This is a large and complex problem which will *not* easily be solved.

The Case for or Against Diagnostic and Therapeutic Sexism

Ruth B. Hoppe

Complex processes of sex bias and sex-role stereotyping in all likelihood detract from the health care received by both men and women. However, to the extent that sex bias in health care does exist, the implications for women are probably greater given that most physicians are men and well over half of all patients are women. When one explores the medical literature, there are strong hints that the potential for diagnostic and therapeutic sexism exists, but there is very little, if any, direct evidence. In most instances where sexism is cited as an explanation for the behavior of health professionals toward women, there are other equally valid explanations. For example, women receive nearly two-thirds of the prescriptions for psychoactive drugs (such as minor tranquilizers like Valium and Librium), suggesting that, because of therapeutic sexism, their symptoms may have been seen as psychologically based and treated accordingly, at a rate different from men.[1] Such a view is supported by the fact that male psychiatrists have been noted to prescribe drugs more frequently if the patient is a woman (37% versus 28%), and male psychiatrists more often prescribe drugs than do female psychiatrists.[2] On the other hand, women have a greater frequency of visits to physicians, and *any* patient's visit to a physician is likely to result in a prescription for a drug. Furthermore, women more frequently report anxiety, stress and diffuse symptoms for which such drugs were developed, perhaps due to differences in actual levels of anxiety and stress, or due to differences in acknowledging the presence of such symptoms. Finally, when use of non-prescription,

Presented at the DMH Women's Task Force Public Forum, "Treatment of the Female Client—Part I," Detroit, Michigan, January 15, 1981.

Ruth Hoppe is a general internist and Associate Professor in the Department of Medicine at Michigan State University's College of Human Medicine, East Lansing, Michigan.

over-the-counter drug use is analyzed, women also use more than men.[3]

Another example is surgical treatment for coronary artery disease, the problem that causes heart attacks, which affects many more men in our country than women. The decision to use surgery or medical treatment for this problem is highly controversial and highly variable among physicians. However, the number of men who receive the surgical approach is beyond the epidemiologic preponderance of coronary artery disease in men, at least by those who report their results in the medical literature.[5] There are many reasons that might be ascribed to this difference, one of which is sexist therapeutics. Another reason might be that the medical literature is dominated by studies from Veterans' Administration hospitals which treat predominantly male patients.

A final example might be the notorious infrequency of breast examination that ought to be done as part of the routine performance of general physical examinations. A survey in 1973 revealed that 25% of women 65 and older had never had a breast examination despite the fact that breast cancer is the number two killer of women.[6] Now again, there might be other explanations. For example, most male physicians require a female attendant when they examine female breasts and female genitalia, and perhaps the pace in a busy physician's office precludes that kind of attendance, and therefore the examination isn't done. Or, in 1973, women were perhaps not yet in the habit of seeking out routine, gynecologic care of which a breast examination would be a part.

Despite the lack of direct evidence and the availability of alternative explanations for seemingly sexist interventions, there are some areas which should cause concern. One area relates to the general social status of women and the cultural attitudes which then influence the response to these women when they become patients. As reflected in casual comments,[7] medical textbooks[4] and medical advertising,[9] women are generally portrayed as having trivial complaints or as having symptoms that are largely psychological in origin and occasionally as being frankly hysterical. (It is interesting to explore the etymology of the word "hysterical," derived from the Greek referring to a uterus wandering around loose and presumably causing psychologic perturbations.) An alarming example of such attitudes is revealed in the language and attitudes of some textbooks which physicians read, particularly gynecologic textbooks. A review of gynecology textbooks published in the period from 1943 to 1972 found the following: 67% of these textbooks proposed that women's interest in sex was primarily for reproductive purposes; 50% of these stated that vaginal orgasm was the only mature female sexual response; and 33% put forth the fact that a majority of women are frigid. [4] Many of these textbooks were written after the Masters and Johnson data were published. Some of the quotes from these texts are illustrative:

> The fundamental urge of women is motherhood balanced by the fact that sexual pleasure is entirely secondary or absent.

> Women are almost universally generally frigid.

> If there had been too much masturbation of the clitoris it may be reluctant to abandon control, or the vagina may be unwilling to accept the combined role of arbiter of sensation and vehicle for reproduction.

And finally,

> An important feature of sex desire in the man is the urge to dominate the women and subjugate her to his will. In a woman, acquiescence to the masterful takes high place.

At the very least, such statements reflect a woeful lack of knowledge about women patients and their problems. At the worst, they reflect attitudes pernicious to the delivery of optimal health care. Another example which perhaps mirrors that contained in some medical textbooks is advertising in medical journals. A recent formal analysis of four commonly read and widely distributed medical journals found some interesting trends. One is that advertisements for psychoactive drugs commonly portray the patient as being female, whereas advertisements for non-psychoactive drugs (cold medicines, diabetes medicine, etc.) portray the patient as being male. Presumably men have real, organic diseases and women unphysiologic and perhaps unreal, complaints. Another finding was that the medical problems of women were often shown to be of irritation to others. One rather vivid example has a picture of a family gathered around a table, focusing on the woman. The caption beneath the ad says, "Treat one, six people benefit."[9] Such advertising no doubt reflects attitudes that exist in our culture about women, and cannot be attributed to clinicians alone. However, professionals can perpetuate these stereotypes under the guise of "expert" opinion which can in turn exert a powerful influence on individual care settings as well as in medical education and health policy arenas. Perhaps even the long waits in doctors' waiting rooms are an example of doctors having less than appropriate respect for the time commitments of their patients; the doctors on the one hand being men, and the patients, on the other, being women.

A second area with potential for diagnostic and therapeutic sexism relates to illnesses and conditions experienced by women as a result of their unique reproductive biology. Five such conditions include primary dysmenorrhea (pain with menstruation), premenstrual tension, nausea of pregnancy, pain in labor, and menopause with its associated constellation of symptoms. All these conditions share the fact that men (and hence the majority of those health professionals who treat them) never experience the symptoms. Another feature common to these subjects is the persistence, despite scientific evidence to the contrary, of the belief that they are caused by or aggravated by psychogenic factors. Menstrual pain, for example, is a well-defined entity affecting the majority of women to some extent, some severely. Its presence seems to depend wholly on the occurrence of ovulation and more recently, a hormonal basis has been outlined. Despite these facts, many physicians still view dysmenorrhea as a psychogenic problem, afflicting the "high-strung" or nervous female, being an excuse to avoid unpleasant activities, or merely, "always secondary to an emotional problem."[10]

Menopausal symptoms are another example of how there appears to have been perseverance of experience, folklore, and down-right illogical and incorrect thinking that has continued well beyond the generation of scientific facts. The persistence of damaging and untrue beliefs in the face of scientific evidence is one way of defining prejudice. With menopause, there are some deeply ingrained attitudes, supporting the idea that women are at the mercy of their uteruses. Lydia Pinkham's Vegetable Compound was used to treat female complaints many years ago. An advertisement from that era shows a woman with a furrowed brow about to be given the compound with a caption which says, "Don't blame her." That is, this woman is having a number of female complaints emanating from her unique biology for which *she* is really not at fault. One 19th century physician thought that women decayed after menopause starting with the uterus and spreading out from there. Some Victorian physicians thought that the severity of the menopausal syndrome was due to prior indiscretions, usually of a sexual nature.

We like to think that we are more enlightened in the 1980s, but components of these attitudes exist today and are part of some of the myths and the fears generated in women regarding menopause. To some degree, we are still dealing with what may be called the paradox of menopause. The paradox is this: on the one hand, women generate physiological symptoms, the hot flash, for example, which in the past has been thought to have a psychological basis and it has been treated as if it were a psychological complaint. Today, most physicians probably understand the physiological basis of the hot flash, but many may still feel that the severity of the complaints that surround it are largely psychologically-based rather than physiological. To the extent this is true and sets the stage for these physiologically-based symptoms to be ignored or inappropriately treated with psychoactive medications. The other side is even more worrisome, where psychological problems are addressed with physiologic therapy. Many middle-aged women have problems dealing with common difficulties of that age period, for example, adapting to aging and to changes in role, which for some women are profound. When these events produce symptoms and happen to coincide with the cessation of menstruation, they are thought to have a physical basis and are often treated physiologically with estrogen replacement therapy. Another advertisement depicts this process rather graphically: a menopausal lady with lovely gray hair is shown holding a vase of roses. The roses are wilted and the entire picture is tremendously out of focus. This is an advertisement for Premarin and the lady who is out of focus is irritable, fatigued, and not sleeping well. The advertisement appears to be suggesting that *all* these symptoms (including her dead roses!) would be improved by estrogen replacement therapy. This type of advertising is inappropriate for three reasons. First, there is no scientific evidence that the non-specific symptoms of menopause are helped by estrogen. There are only three benefits that are thought to be offered by estrogen replacement therapy: relief of the hot flash, relief of the drying of genital tissue that occurs as a result of estrogen lack, and slowing of the softening of bones that occurs in all people, women faster than men. These are well-documented benefits of estrogen therapy, but there is no scientific evidence that the non-specific symptoms (such as sleeplessness, fatigue, irritability) sometimes seen in women in this age group are helped by estrogen. A second reason is that for some women, particularly those who have intact uteruses, estrogen replacement has some risks, and the decision to embark on therapy needs to carefully weigh the benefits and the risks. Finally, it is inappropriate because it fails to deal directly with the psychosocial issues of women in middle age so that the real sources of these symptoms are once again ignored or inappropriately treated.

There are surgical issues related to the reproductive biology of women which at the very least have been slow to have adequate information generated through the traditional avenue of research and discussion in the medical literature. One has to do with the use of less radical surgery for breast cancer. Another relates to changing indications for hysterectomy, in part a result of the feeling that there has been overuse of this procedure in the past. Finally, the tripling in the rate of Caesarean sections during the decade of the 1970s and in general, a more technologic approach to childbirth has occurred despite concerns raised by women and despite no clear relationship, in the aggregate, of these procedures to improved maternal or fetal health.[11]

Clearly, some of these issues are already being explored. The women's movement has obviously been instrumental in altering some societal attitudes and in challenging traditional views. Hysterectomy rates are down and we *are* questioning reasons for hysterectomies being performed. Much attention has been given in the medical literature, particularly the surgical literature, about what is the most appropriate surgical operation for breast cancer. Should it be a radical operation which removes the entire breast and large amounts of tissue of the chest wall or a simple procedure removing just the lump? We don't have firm answers to these questions, but we are looking at them. At long last, a physiologic basis for the pain of menstruation has been defined and the antagonism of this physiologic basis has worked its way into common medical practice. There are clues to a physiologic basis of severe premenstrual tension, although a consistently effective form of therapy remains elusive. The complex weighing of the benefits and risk of estrogen replacement therapy has been under active recent investigation. Finally, there are increasing numbers of women in medical schools which is beginning to have an effect on the numbers of women in practice. In 1970, 7.6% of all practicing physicians were women, and 10% of medical students were women. By 1980, these numbers had risen to 12% and 25% respectively.[12] There is anecdotal evidence which suggests that these women are beginning to make an impact on the behaviors and, hopefully, attitudes of their male colleagues.

There is much more that could be done, particularly in the education and information dissemination areas. First would be to promote patient education. There are materials available at federal and state levels about women's medical problems that need to be shared and perhaps rewritten in languages and at reading levels to reach a larger portion of the population. Another educational area is the curricula of health classes both in the secondary and elementary school levels which can be examined to ensure that appropriate issues are identified for inclusion and that appropriate kinds of information and texts are being used. Secondly, we need to promote personal advocacy in health care. We need to teach patients, and particularly women patients, how to advocate for their own best interest in receiving health care: that has to do with expecting informed consent and learning how to elicit informed consent. Interest groups have been organized to serve this purpose. Third, we need to challenge pharmaceutical companies to engage in more responsible advertising. This could be done by health care leaders and consumers, using positive and negative feedback strategies. A fourth need is to stimulate research. Research questions need to be better formulated and monies offered to address questions which still require better definition and better scientific understanding. And finally, the process of educating physicians will be enhanced by support of increased numbers of women in medical schools and also seeing that women's health topics are given serious and appropriate treatment in curricula. For example, the National Council on Alcoholism sponsors career teachers whereby faculty members are funded in medical schools and given a responsibility to teach about alcoholism. Perhaps teaching about women's health care could be similarly funded and promulgated in medical schools.

To summarize, an in-depth review of these issues and others leads one to conclude that the health care of women has been hampered by inadequate information, prolonged persistence of incorrect attitudes in the face of contrary evidence, and incursion into health care of societal attitudes about women which are stereotyped and constrained by narrow role definitions. We need much more information about women's health problems and their optimal management.

This needs to be generated with a scientific basis: not to prove that sexism in health care exists, but to improve the health status and the health care of women.

REFERENCES

1. Carmen, E., Russo, N.F. and Miller J.B. Inequality and Woman's Mental Health: An overview. *American Journal of Psychiatry, 138:*10, 1981.

2. Cypress, B.K. Characteristics of Visits to Female and Male Physicians. *The National Ambulatory Medical Care Survey,* United States, 1977. Hyattsville, MD, National Center for Health Statistics, 1980.

3. Cypress, *Ibid.*

4. Scully, D. and Bart, P. A Funny Thing Happened on the Way to the Orifice: Woman in Gynecology Textbooks. *American Journal of Sociology, 78:*1045, 1973.

5. Lawrie, G.M. and Morris, G.C. Survival After Coronary Artery Bypass Surgery in Specific Patient Groups. *Circulation* 65 (Supp II):43, 1982.

6. Women and Health United States, 1980. *Public Health Reports Supplement,* September-October, 1980, 4-8b.

7. Howel, M.D. Doctor Women, *New England Journal of Medicine, 291:*303, 1974.

8. Scully, *Ibid.*

9. Prather, I. and Fidell, S. Sex Differences in the Content and Style of Medical Advertisements, *Social Science in Medicine, 9:*23, 1975.

10. Lennane, K.J. and Lennane, R.J. Alleged Psychogenic Disorders in Women–A Possible Manifestation of Sexual Prejudice, *New England Journal of Medicine, 288:*288, 1973.

11. Phillips, R.N., Thornton, J. and Gleicher, N. Physician Bias in Caesarean Sections. *Journal of the American Medical Association, 248:*1082, 1982.

12. Braslow, J.B. and Heins, M. Women in Medical Education–A Decade of Change. *New England Journal of Medicine, 304:*1129, 1981.

Case Study:
Women and the Health Care System—
Patients or Victims?

Carol T. Mowbray

In two years she would be a lawyer—a member of the Bar. It was true that she still had a year of law courses to complete and the Michigan Bar Exam to pass, but the last year of law school was relatively easy and she had never had trouble with standardized examinations—her grades were good. With this goal in mind, her past stressful experiences over the last ten years seemed minimal. There had been a divorce and a number of people close to her had died; she still had unreasonable fears of flunking out of law school despite the good grades. Recently, though, things were bothering her more—there was some litigation over family property which had arisen. She was having more and more trouble sleeping. This stress reaction had appeared before, but it was never serious. Now she felt that, on the verge of future success, she should do something about it. She saw her doctor who prescribed a tranquilizer (Atavan) and sleeping pills (along with ongoing antihistamines). Although her doctor advised her that all these medications could be taken together, she was reluctant to do so and never got the sleeping pills.

Things got worse—irritability, trembling, trouble with her eyes and, worst of all, no sleep. She felt hyped up all the time. Although she thought she looked like a "mental case," she ignored her problem, thinking that these symptoms were explainable stress reactions to her exams. But when exams were over, the conditions still persisted. After more than eight weeks went by, she returned to her doctor. Her doctor conducted no physical examination or medication review—he had seen cases like this before. Women with basic-

Dr. Mowbray is a psychologist, Chair of the Michigan Women's Task Force, and Director of Research and Evaluation in the Michigan Department of Mental Health.

ally hysterical personalities who take on too much and wind up with nervous breakdowns. Was there any mental illness in her family? She thought maybe a once-removed cousin. Doctor S. told her that obviously she had mental problems, needed psychiatric help, and there was nothing more he could do.

Mentally ill? Could it be true? A doctor must know what he is talking about. Confusion. What to do? Three or four days without any sleep at all. Had to get away. It was the people here in this city. And stop taking the medicine. Part of a plot.

So she went to visit a friend in Detroit. No help. Bizarre behavior. Nearly drove them crazy. Clothes dirty. Body odor. Wild—running through the house. Screaming all the time.

Finally in the middle of one night, her friends could take no more and drove her to the hospital emergency room. They needed sleep too. She managed to blurt out a story to a doctor there. A foreign woman. Could the doctor understand her? How could she when she could hardly speak English herself! The woman told her her blood pressure was high and she was having paranoid ideas. But she couldn't be admitted then. All they could do was let her stay the night and give her something to let her sleep. A mild sedative—but the container said Mellaril.

Really afraid. Things got worse. WIDE AWAKE. Couldn't breathe. Where's the doctor?

The doctor told her she was a hard-to-manage patient, that she would have to calm down and stay in the bed.

Hold on. Wait until morning. The hours slowly ticked away.

Up in the morning, she felt better, more coherent. I want to see my chart. What have you done to me? I want to leave.

NO! NO! NO! Go to the Crisis Center. You need help but we can't do it here.

She called a friend to drive her back to her car. On the way back home, her mouth was paralyzed with dryness; she was freaking out, terrorized. Once at home she stepped into a warm shower to relax and instead felt numbness through her whole body. She was convinced they had done something to her. Hyperventilating, she drove herself to the local emergency room. A psychologist there said she was mostly scared from her experience and talked to her for three hours, calming her down.

Back at home, a cup of coffee again set her off. She was stuttering, pacing the floor, and afraid to be alone.

I must be crazy. I need help.

She drove to the community psychiatric unit and voluntarily admitted herself. The nurse on her ward told her, "I'm going to warn you, we have rules here. You're on the open end. If you get agitated, we'll put you on Thorazine and lock you up."

She was now so worried about what was happening to her she still didn't sleep. Four days without sleep. And the woman in her room with her was moaning all night long. The woman said it was because the doctor had put her on tranquilizers. It must be part of the plot. Escape. Leave the hospital.

So she got out and went to see some of her friends. But that didn't help either. Go back to the hospital, they said. You need help. And she was scared again. Really afraid. Afraid of hyperventilating and not being able to stop. Afraid of being out of control, of losing herself forever. Afraid of dying.

They called the police, she wouldn't get in their car. A second police car had to come to help.

This time when she went into the hospital it seemed like everyone was really nice to her. She spent the whole day in group therapy. She felt better and safer, but still not safe enough to accept any of the medications.

The group therapy began to get boring. Nothing to do but kids' games. Still she was not sleeping much. The psychiatrist wanted to get her an antipsychotic for her paranoia and, if not that, a tranquilizer like Valium. She felt like she was in prison. Why wouldn't they let her go? What was the matter with her? What caused these problems? She complained a lot to get the answers to these questions and was then released the next day.

Three months later, her experience still haunted her. She still was not really better. There seemed to be many more conflicts with people than before. She exploded and lost her temper easily. *Was* she crazy—or what?

SUMMARY

Stress and tension seemed to be the immediate causes of this woman's sleeping problems. Instead of helping her deal with the stresses through her own resources, her family doctor applied a bandaid. This time the bandaid did not cover up the problem but made it worse. She experienced an adverse, opposite reaction to the tranquilizer. Rather than identifying the medication as the obvious cause of her worsening condition, her doctor played psychiatrist and assumed her problems were rooted in her personality and family history.

When she got still worse, she attempted to get away and discontinue her medication. A withdrawal reaction occurred. Then Emergency Room admission. The emergency room dealt with this case based on the woman's disheveled, dirty condition and diagnosed a psychotic episode without seriously examining the history of the problem or alternative treatment. With antipsychotic medications given, more adverse reactions occurred, new symptoms emerged.

Inpatient treatment is not democratic, but sometimes drawing some attention to yourself does bring improvements. Although her second admission to the local hospital was less threatening, treatment options were still limited, or ineffective, and use of medications was automatically pushed.

The after-effects of this one experience were still felt many months later. And if psychiatric problems ever occur in the future, professionals will deal with this woman as a repeater—on her way to chronic mental illness—all because of reactions to medications that should *never* have occurred and even when they did occur were dealt with inappropriately. There may be a potential for serious, irreversible damage. And what would have happened to her if she had ignored her own common sense and continued to take the medications which the doctors pushed her to take? Was this woman the patient or the victim of these doctors and the health care system?

Summary and Recommendations: Medical Treatment and Medication Practices

One of our doctors in the ghetto tells the story of a patient who appears to be exhausted. She tells the doctor that she doesn't sleep well at night. While an ignorant doctor would prescribe a sleeping pill, a sensitive one first asks, 'Why?' The woman then can explain that the rats crawl into her baby's crib if she's not awake to chase them away.

Selma Goode (1980)

A woman who presents a physician with 'pain' is likely to be told the pain is not a significant problem, and if she is 'worried' by the pain, she needs something for her nerves, or she needs counseling. Here is a recent instance: The employed mother of two preschoolers presented abdominal and back pains numerous times. Her HMO refused to address these problems and refused to authorize her to seek outside assistance. Instead, they referred her to their mental health unit and she complied in an effort to prove her sanity so that the pains would be accepted as legitimate. This proved impossible. To the HMO staff her written attempts to obtain referral clearly demonstrated her anger (neurosis, conversion hysteria, functional disorder). After considerable expense, duodenal ulcers, hiatal hernia, deformed antrum (cause unknown) and a high probability of gallstones were discovered. Of course, the HMO is not liable since they did not 'authorize' the expenditures. They maintained the anger of this woman was clearly pathological and required treatment, while the presenting symptoms of pain were irrelevant. I know this because this person was me.

Testimony submitted to the Women's Task Force
(1980)

It is becoming increasingly clear that health services available to women greatly need improvement. The same sexual prejudices that prevail in society in general are pervasive in health care settings. Physicians are conservative in their notions about women's roles in society and reportedly feel that women display more mental disorders and are less stoic than men during illness. As a whole, physicians expect women to be more "difficult" patients (Fidell, 1977).

A physician's stereotypic biases can be extremely detrimental to women's physiological and psychological health. For example, often misdiagnoses occur when women's genuine physiological complaints are interpreted by physicians as "nerves," psychosomatic complaints, or mental health problems. Once such a label is applied, the remainder of the patient's remarks are likely to be ignored.

Women are experiencing two major problems with their physicians—misdiagnoses and over-medication. These problems interact in that when valid physical symptoms are misdiagnosed as mental health problems or suppressed by medication, they can then exacerbate into something worse.

While it is true according to research that men and women present their symptoms to physicians differently (Zola, 1966), this alone does not explain the prevalence of diagnostic sexism. Even medical texts have portrayed women as having problems that have extensive psychological components.

For disorders congruent with sex role stereotyping (i.e., depression, conversion hysteria and phobias), women show higher rates of service utilization than do men (Russo and VandenBos, 1980) and are reported by physicians to have more psychiatric problems, psychosomatic complaints, and unexplained symptoms (Kravits, 1975). Unfortunately, depression and other emotional problems are often viewed as "female" problems about which little can be done other than through medication. But the identification and treatment of disorders associated with a special stigma for women require a high level of expertise, sensitivity and individuation that has been lacking on the part of physicians.

These facts have a special meaning for poor women. Frequently, when poor women complain to their doctors about any kind of unpleasant feelings, they get prescriptions for tranquilizers. It is a rare medical doctor who recognizes and responds adequately to mental health problems. It has been previously noted that many of the poor in our country are women and a growing percentage are older women. Many of the elderly who must reside in nursing homes are over-medicated and that translates into mental health problems. In the elderly, psychiatric problems are actually *caused* by medication abuses and polypharmacy in many cases. And this becomes a woman's issue since the majority of the elderly population—especially those in psychiatric hospitals—are women.

The statistics at the national level on the problem of over-medication, especially involving psychotropic drugs are alarming (Fidell, 1977). On the state level, two to three hundred thousand persons in Michigan use prescription drugs, and two-thirds of these are women (Ryan, 1981). For large numbers of these women, feelings of powerlessness, helplessness and dependency may be intensified through use of psychotropic drugs. Drugs can place women in a sick role and facilitate a reduction in symptoms rather than affect the causative factors.

The rate of prescribing psychotropic drugs to women also raises questions concerning the dangers of taking certain mental health problems to physicians. Although many problems have social/psychological roots, doctors are, after all, trained to dispense *medicine.* Unfortunately, psychotropic drugs have become likely remedies to prescribe to patients with complex social problems which busy physicians don't have time for.

The rueful fact remains that if a woman is drugged into conformity, then society does not have to deal with her cries of inequality. The Women's Task Force recommends that the issue of over-medication of women must be thoroughly investigated and addressed. Medication may suppress positive coping strategies of women, especially for those already experiencing a stressful life event, and may affect a woman's ability to function both at work and at home. In addition, physicians must keep in mind that psychological effects from use of psychotropic drugs can become very serious. Risks incurred from possible side effects may far outweigh the possible benefits for many women.

This is not to say that physicians are completely to blame for the sexual prejudices and over-medication practices found in health settings today. Physicians, after all, are products of their medical training and socialization, and must be cautioned to guard against making diagnoses based upon their role expectations for their female patients. This training responsibility must be assumed by medical schools. However, medical schools are just beginning to have larger numbers of women medical students,* and at this point few women physicians are doing the training.

Efforts of medical schools to revise their curricula can be a successful remedy to these problems. Future medical training must also include strategies for more effective communication between patients and doctors. Physicians must be trained to become more sensitive to all socioeconomic and cultural groups of women they serve. Communication between patient and physician is likely to be poor when there are language barriers. Cultural and ethnic differences in the definition of the ''sick role'' additionally complicate communications by minority women.

After completion of medical training, many doctors rely on medical journals for much of their current information. But medical journals also promote many stereotypic notions about women and their needs and they often rely on funds from advertising by drug companies. The selling of psychotropic drugs is big business and many have vested interests in a continuation of the current rates of consumption.

The key to resolving these issues may lie in better education. Not only should physicians be better prepared to

---

*According to the Michigan Office of Health and Medical Affairs, the proportion of females to males in Michigan's four medical schools is 29% to 71% respectively.

understand their female patients, but patient education must be encouraged and promoted. The model of patient passivity must be replaced by one supporting the active participation of both patient and physician. Much of the knowledge about women's physical and psychological health that was formerly esoteric is now becoming demystified. It is time for all of those involved in the health care profession to become more responsive to women's needs and for women to take a more active role in asserting what is appropriate treatment.

RECOMMENDATIONS

A. Administration of Mental Health Services

1. Health curriculums in primary and secondary schools should be thoroughly reviewed to identify inaccuracies concerning women's health problems.
2. Because of the alarming statistics that have surfaced relating to over-medication and its impact on women's mental health, prescribing practices of physicians in the public mental health system should also be reviewed.

B. Training Issues

1. Because of evidence that physicians tend to prescribe psychoactive drugs to women because of stereotypic biases, university medical schools and professional organizations must educate current students and alumni about the harm and impact of over-medication and the too permissive use of medication. These practices and trends must change if women's mental health is to be promoted.
2. Medical schools must promote physician's consciousness of women's treatment issues by encouraging and supporting increased numbers of women in medical schools, including more women in faculty positions and educating physicians to be more knowledgeable of women's health issues, e.g., dysmenorrhea,

menopause, nausea of pregnancy, and inappropriate radical surgery for breast cancer or hysterectomy.

3. Medical schools should increase consciousness of sexism in treatment issues of women and should examine the attitudes and language of medical textbooks, especially in gynecology.
4. Case material presented and literature reviewed on the overuse and misuse of drugs indicate a pervasive over-tranquilizing of women. Continuing medical education programs should address these issues. Medical societies should take action to investigate and remediate practices of tranquilization where doctors assume women have emotional problems rather than properly identifying a physical basis for their complaints. Depression is still undertreated, misdiagnosed and/or mistreated with valium.

C. Public Policy Support

1. Understanding that existing sex biases in medical advertisements can contribute to incorrect attitudes about women and their illness, pharmaceutical houses should be encouraged to eliminate offensive, sexist advertising. Medical societies and medical doctors are encouraged to take action by not purchasing those journals or drugs whose advertising promotes this sex bias.
2. Women's resource centers and other local resource groups must encourage women to advocate for their own best interest in order to prevent misdiagnoses or inappropriate diagnoses of physical ailments. Activities of these groups should include the collection and dissemination of accurate information, providing workshops for women so that they can learn to be more assertive with medical professionals vis-à-vis being responsible for giving truly informed consent, and providing women with knowledge about self-care and a better awareness of their health status.
3. In order to provide more and better scientific information on the still neglected area of women's medical problems, efforts should be undertaken by universi-

ties and the Federal government to stimulate more high quality research. Universities must also make an effort to fill more faculty positions with people who have done or have interest in research on women's health and medical problems.

4. The use of anti-trust laws to decrease physician dominance and allow and fund other health care providers to practice at the level of their education should be explored. Consumers often have to choose a physician because they do not have open access to alternative providers.

SECTION 5:
INNOVATIVE MENTAL HEALTH
TREATMENT ALTERNATIVES
FOR WOMEN:
THE EVIDENCE

FEMINIST THERAPY

In the last two decades, American society has undergone real changes in its attitudes about the role of women. Some mental health clinicians have re-examined their attitudes toward appropriate sex-role behaviors for women and begun a process of redefining what constitutes healthy and unhealthy behaviors, which goes beyond confining stereotypic role definitions to include behaviors previously thought to be deviant or unhealthy. Feminist therapy or non-sexist therapy is a non-traditional approach to the treatment of women, focusing on the relationship between the socialization of women and their mental health problems. (This chapter will follow the practice of most sources to not differentiate the two—although Franks (1979) makes the distinction that feminist therapy identifies a sociopolitical component to therapy while non-sexist therapy focuses on the individual apart from sex-role stereotypes.)

A number of definitions of feminist therapy have been put forth. One basic assumption to the approach is that ''ideology, social structure, and behavior are inextricably woven'' (Brodsky and Hare-Mustin, 1980, p. 242) and that there is a basic harmful conflict between the norms of our social institutions and the expectations and social reality of women's

149

behavior within those norms. Feminist therapy is a type of counseling that frees women from traditional sex role stereotypes, minimizes the differences in power between the therapist and the client, and emphasizes a person's right to self-actualization (President's Commission on Mental Health, 1978).

In a practical sense this means that the feminist therapist disclaims herself as an "expert" on the client's problems. Rather, the client is viewed "as an individual with a unique set of personal problems and a related set of problems resulting from the individual's interacting with society" (Naierman, 1979, p. 13). An important treatment aspect of this model is facilitating the expression of anger—seen by some as the establishment of women's power and by others as an important factor in depression, highly prevalent among women. Another important aspect is elimination of the dominant-submissive role in the therapist-client relationship and an emphasis on power and autonomy. The intended outcome of feminist therapy is helping the woman to achieve her own emotional and human potential, regardless of sex-role stereotypes. Very little empirical work has been done testing outcome differences between female and male clients when treatment is focused on problems resulting from socialization rather than on pathology, although we know that therapists' values appear to have more influence on outcome than demographic variables (Parloff et al., 1978) and that feminist mental health therapists view their clients as healthier (that is, stronger and less ill) than traditional therapists (Bosma, 1975).

Joan Israel, herself a feminist therapist, presents two case histories—useful because they demonstrate the significance of the model not only for treating women, but the great potential for treatment of men.

> Alice is a woman in her late 30s, divorced for about five years, with custody of her four children, now 18, 16, 10 and 8. After the birth of her last child, Alice went back to school to become an occupational therapist, a profession she found very satisfying. She had come from a traditional middle-class family and had married a successful businessman at age 18. She said

she had never really loved her former husband but had married him because of pressure from her parents (''he was a good catch''). She had a very traditional marriage, having complete responsibility for the children's care. Her former husband had on occasion given lip service to the idea of sharing this responsibility. About a year ago, Alice came for help because she felt she wanted to give up permanent custody of the children to her husband. She was tired, irritable, had developed a relationship with another man. She felt that her children had two parents and that their father had an equal responsibility toward their care. The children had a good relationship with their father, and he responded positively to Alice's suggestion that he take over custody. He could provide better material and emotional support for them at this time. She was drained. She would like to take the children on weekends—to be the ''fun parent.'' She felt very guilty, however, and wanted to make sure she was doing the right thing. Years ago, acting on this would have been unusual, and Alice would have been thought of as an uncaring person and an unfit mother. As we explored her feelings, it was clear that she had indeed been a good mother. I reinforced this after careful examination of how she had related to her children over the years. Her present resentment grew out of the years she had spent renouncing the gratification of her own reasonable needs in favor of the needs of others.

Jim F. was an unmarried 20-year-old undergraduate student when he first came to see me three years ago. He had heard me speak at a round table seminar on feminist therapy at a professional meeting. He worked in a local social welfare agency. His presenting problem was the handling of sporadic outbursts of violent anger. He was also troubled by his relationship to his father, a high ranking politician whom he admired but from whom he felt distance and disapproval. Jim never felt he was masculine enough to please his father. He alternated between trying to please him (by playing football, building up his body, doing carpentry) and being angry that his father didn't love and accept him as he was. He was much closer to his mother, a warm, affectionate, non-critical woman who acted as a buffer between Jim and his father. Jim had some close friends who were homosexual, but he never felt conflicted about his own sexuality. Jim had difficulty in his long-term relationships with women. He realized that he expected women to be like his mother so that he could continue playing the little boy. This invariably led to his disappointment both in women and in himself, and to the termination of the relationships. Interestingly enough, he worked out his violence rather easily after recognizing that it was both self-destructive and an expression of hostility toward his father. As he recognized the nature of his conflicts, and as he gained approval from me for increased emotional self-reliance, Jim developed more self-confidence and maturity. He was then able to approach his father in confrontational but friendly talks, discussing what was bothering him and what in their relationship he would like to change. In accepting the fact that he could be sensitive and expressive and at the same time mature, Jim developed a conception of what a man is that is very different from that of his father. He will have more room to include a variety of feelings in his conception of the male image. (Israel, 1979, p. 20)

Feminist therapy is still seen as political, threatening, and of questionable legitimacy, so professionally identifying oneself as a feminist therapist can be an act of courage (Fibel, 1976).

SELF-HELP AND SUPPORT GROUPS

Self-help groups also focus less on pathology and more on the individual's healthy, functioning side. Groups provide safe, "non-sick" settings for individuals to work on their mental health problems while avoiding cultural inhibitions about seeking help and the stigmatizing label as a mental health client.

Group support is helpful in allowing women to see that they are not alone in their problems, to discover that such problems may be caused more by their circumstances than their own faults and deficits, and to find solutions. The role of support in alleviating or preventing mental health problems has only been peripherally established. For instance, compared to those who do not talk to others when worried, talkers tend to be lower in ill health, higher in happiness, less likely to be depressed and higher in self-esteem (Veroff et al., 1981). At this point in time, scientific evaluations of the effects of self-help or support groups on mental health problems are not adequate to *establish* effectiveness. However, case studies and small scale evaluations have produced some impressive results.

An outstanding non-traditional program is the Elizabeth Stone House, located in Jamaica Plain, Massachusetts. Created by former mental patients, paraprofessionals and feminists as a self-help refuge in the community, its primary goal has been to provide services to emotionally distressed Boston area women and their children. It is a program combining low-cost residential services with advocacy and support for resolving practical and emotional problems. It provides an alternative for women who are in distress due to pressures and life stressors. The users of the Elizabeth Stone house are former mental patients, victims of violence, mothers living with or away from their children, women involved with the criminal justice system, former and recovering drug and alcohol addicts, and women making major transitions in their lives.

The philosophy of the house is to help yourself. Women residents share the responsibilities of running the house while also taking time to meet in groups to talk about emotional difficulties and practical problems, such as how to get a job or where to look for an apartment. The staff members of the house are not professionals. Sometimes they are former mental health clients, but the main criteria for the staff selection is an emphasis on empathy, practicality and self-help. While the house is supported by grants, the women themselves must pay for rent and food. The underlying philosophy is that when women feel secure and safe enough, they can make important changes for themselves.

While the Elizabeth Stone House began as a political group hoping to change the structure of the mental health establishment (which they have not succeeded in doing), they nevertheless have helped many low income women.

> . . . At the Stone House, practical issues such as housing, jobs, finances, educational/vocational training are addressed and resolved through staff counseling and advocacy. Women in the program provide each other with emotional support. Through self-help and mutual support women gain the strength to work through and resolve their practical and emotional problems. (Belle, 1982)

The house can accommodate 21 women and children and over the past eight years has helped more than 700 poor, emotionally distressed women and their children.

Transition House in Cambridge, Massachusetts is another type of self-help residence that provides temporary refuge for battered women and their children. Their philosophy is that women in a non-violent and supportive environment will develop their individual and collective strengths for helping themselves and each other. It provides such services as shelter for four to six weeks, a 24-hour crisis line, child care assistance, parenting support groups, battered women support groups, and a legal action committee.

Another type of self-help group was begun in Michigan as a pilot mental health prevention project on stress management with low income women who constituted a large proportion of mental health consumers (see the Perspective chapter by Marciniak). The program is intended to help women increase self-esteem, improve interpersonal relationships, develop additional social supports, increase strategies available to them to manage stress, and strengthen their beliefs that they are capable of taking control of their own lives.

The Department of Social Services refers women who they believe to be at risk for developing stress-related problems, but are not yet exhibiting severe symptoms. Referred women may eventually become part of a group of eight to fourteen which meets three hours a week for ten consecutive weeks at a downtown church. Each ten-week workshop is divided into three components: self-esteem, decision-making and life planning, and stress management. Child care and transportation are provided. A rigorous evaluation, using an experimental design, has established the effectiveness of this intervention, especially on depressive feelings. In addition, the women like the workshop and feel that it improves their attitude, self-concept and ability to cope.

CONCLUSION

Traditional psychotherapy is often founded on common basic assumptions which "defy, distort or devalue the female experience in a male-dominated culture" (Brodsky and Hare-Mustin, 1980, p. 211). Cultural contexts cannot be excluded from the world of therapy. Non-traditional approaches to therapy are specifically trying to provide alternatives. However, little has been done to evaluate the effectiveness of the wide range of professional and non-professional therapeutic and self-help services offered by women's centers, feminist agencies, or mental health providers. Research directed toward the full range of innovative therapeutic approaches for women should be a priority. Results could provide a better basis for linkages and referrals between mental health service providers and other agencies and groups. Establishing the effectiveness of these approaches will enable women to have far more choices available to them as more service providers become aware and convinced of their worth.

The perspectives that follow present the diversity of innovative mental health treatment alternatives for women: Joan Israel's philosophy and practice of feminist therapy, a fuller presentation of the operation and outcomes of the Stress Management Workshop for low-income women, and, finally, a description of how a women's resource center provides support and services addressing women's mental health problems.

Feminist Therapy

Joan Israel

I am a feminist therapist. It's no surprise to me!—and it seemed inevitable—although there was no terminology to describe it years ago. My values could have always been described as feminist, mainly because my mother encouraged me and my two sisters not only to do well in school, but to be independent, not to appear dumb in front of boys, and to speak up. This resulted in feeling comfortable enough as I grew older to ask boys/men out on "dates"—something that must have seemed strange in the 1950s. Thus, when the women's movement in the form of NOW appeared on the scene in the late 1960s, that famous "aha" occurred for me as it did for so many other women.

I was married, had two young children and had been working as a social worker and teacher. I went to my first NOW meeting mostly out of curiosity. That curiosity resulted in my becoming a board member, head of the child care committee, president of the local NOW chapter, and later a national board member. It changed my life!—or certainly added a new dimension. At that time the NOW "hot-line" received many calls from women seeking a female psychotherapist who would understand them—they wanted a feminist as a therapist.

I was trained as a traditional social worker and after much personal effort, I developed an approach and understanding based upon my experiences in the women's movement. Some of the aspects that were different were: (1) a more equal relationship between client and therapist (I called people by their first name and they called me by mine); (2) more time spent discussing roles and role expectations; and (3) discussion of the women's movement, if pertinent, and using this as a possible resource. It is important to emphasize

Presentation at the Michigan Department of Mental Health Women's Task Force Public Forum on "Treatment of the Female Client–Part I," Detroit, Michigan, January 15, 1981.

Joan Israel is a social worker who works as a feminist therapist in private practice in Detroit. She also engages in free-lance writing and consultation on women's issues.

157

that no system of values was imposed upon the clients, but that new perceptions and resources were used to help women (and men) understand and improve their sense of themselves.

A few years ago it was stylish to describe oneself as a feminist therapist and professionals jumped on the bandwagon because more and more women were searching out these types of therapists. Traditional psychotherapists give credibility to feminist therapy (although with mixed feelings) because few can ignore the tremendous impact of the women's movement and the changes that have occurred in the last 12 years. Many questions have been raised about relationships, roles, self-concept, etc. Certainly the answers are not simple, but I believe that feminist therapy as an approach is one way to seek sanity in a sometimes insane world.

Some of the changes are: (1) the increasing number of women in the work force, approaching 50 percent (during the last recession, more women kept their jobs than did men because there are more women in low paying service jobs than in production and manufacturing); (2) acceptance of women's work being permanent, not temporary (although our society does little to provide decent, low-cost child care services); (3) later marriages and lower birthrates—which provide for greater mobility and independence of women; and (5) higher divorce rates which lead to a greater increase in one-parent families generally headed by women—which often means carrying a double burden.

There is no doubt in my mind that when significant cultural changes occur, when the old guidelines are not useful, people often feel confused, alienated, and less able to lead satisfactory and happy lives. Feminist therapy, like any therapeutic approach, is not a cure-all, but does provide sensible and useful ways of working with clients.

In her article "Sexism in a Woman's Profession," Kravetz characterizes clinical social work as follows:

> Sex bias and sex role stereotyping pervade clinical theories and literature: psychoanalytic theories, for example, present women as innately passive, dependent, anatomically inferior, and emotionally immature. Motherhood is required as a universal fulfillment. There is increasing pressure to re-enforce that view of women from the conservative segments of our society. Unfortunately, standards used to assess the behavior of female clients and evaluate their psychological distress, and formulate

treatment goals are derived from such concepts. Thus, the prevalence of sex bias in clinical theories is likely to affect practice. (Kravetz, 1976, p. 424)

A way to move away from such practices is to use a set of guidelines developed by the Women's Counselling Group in Brookline, Massachusetts (Radov et al., 1977), based on five components:

1. Feminist therapy assumes in principle that all roles are open to women, although risk taking is greater in non-traditional roles. Very often, how the therapist views the client and how the client views her/himself involves the concept of role expectation and fulfillment. There is greater acceptance of role flexibility, be it the decision to share roles, or not to maintain traditional roles, i.e., get married, have children, etc. In the 1950s-60s, if a woman decided she wanted to have a career, remain single, or not be a mother—she was automatically considered a deviant. There is more tolerance among therapists today. Women were always expected to play it safe in career choices (teacher, nurse, social worker, secretary)—the non-traditional career was viewed as a form of penis envy. Attitudes of therapists are changing on this too.

2. Feminist therapists bring a sociological perspective to their work with women. In doing so, they help women sort out which parts of their behavior have been determined by internalized societal norms and which behavior is in response to current societal pressure. For years, traditional psychotherapeutic concepts have focused predominantly on penis envy or the Oedipal complex and other dynamics arising from early parent/child relationships. Now, women are understanding the way they feel about themselves in a broader context. Also, therapists need to recognize that they have cultural biases and their approach to any client has to be understood in light of her/his own background.

3. Feminist therapists help women develop a new ego ideal. It is important to acknowledge and value the assets of women—nurturing, sensitivity, emphasis on relationships—while at the same time incorporating some of the more aggressive and assertive qualities women have hesitated to develop (a new ego ideal for which there are few role models). As women are making changes in therapy, it is not necessary to copy the male model. It is important to provide opportunity to discuss the challenges and pitfalls of combining positive aspects of male and female role models. Very often, therapists become role models and can provide useful as well as realistic ways

to develop a new ego ideal based upon the client's unique needs and capacities.

4. Feminist therapists strive to help restore a balance of love and work. Usually, men have been helped to work and women to love. It is important for both to do both. It is accepted that women will work, but it is not accepted that men will love or nurture. While women working is seen as economic *necessity,* lip service only is given to the positive aspects of men as caring human beings. This leaves a vacuum in many relationships. Women are becoming tired providing the loving and caring and also part of the family income. Feminist therapy can help clients develop each capacity more realistically.

5. Feminist therapists reassess the value of women's relationships to other women (which may or may not be sexual in nature). Until the women's movement, women not only undervalued themselves, but also other women. It was usually a matter of course that if a woman had a social arrangement with another woman and a man called, she would break her plans and go out with him. Women generally sought male professionals (physicians, lawyers, accountants, etc.) because men were supposed to know more and be more competent. As women's self-esteem and awareness began to rise, so did their seeking out female/feminist professionals. They still have a long way to go, but the fact that the six democratic presidential candidates seriously discuss choosing a woman vice-presidential candidate indicates progress. Maybe next time there will be women presidential candidates—the ultimate symbol of power and authority in our country.

Here are my recommendations for mental health agencies. First, a series of small seminars should be held to explore how people who provide human services to women hold sexist attitudes which get in the way of treating clients. The seminars should include administrators as well as therapists. Case examples would be presented, illustrating specific areas in marriage counseling, working with children, adolescents, older persons, etc. I conducted a successful six-week program for case workers at Jewish Family Services a few years ago—the first of its kind. Other agencies and clinics should provide similar opportunities. Also, resource material dealing with critical times in a woman's life should be made available at agencies and organizations, including libraries and other public information places. More often than not, female issues are trivialized, ignored, and misunderstood, i.e., the myths of menopause.

As much of the current stress emerges from one-parent families headed by women, the mental health system needs to provide help to these parents. This could be in increased homemaker services with homemakers also trained in home maintenance procedures such as simple plumbing or electrical work.

Child care services, high quality, accessible and low cost, have been neglected. Even in these days of cut-backs, creative ways need to be found to provide child care to families.

In the area of women and employment, money issues still need to be discussed in schools, unions, corporations, etc. The state mental health system could devise a media program that would include components and methods to initiate discussion with the goal of increased understanding.

The changing roles of women need continued attention, e.g., the stress of living under a double standard, the pressure for a supermom to do it all, the need for men to share responsibility and power. These are ongoing issues and necessitate ongoing programs both at individual client level and with media attention on a wider basis.

A Stress Management Training Program for Low Income Women

Debbie Marciniak

The Stress Management Training Project targets that group of persons who may be at risk for the development of emotional, cognitive and behavioral problems because they are women, they are poor, they are parenting, and they are not sufficiently buoyed-up by supposedly supportive persons and institutions in the community and in the society at large. The Project was developed jointly by the Ionia County Department of Social Services, the Ionia County Cooperative Extension Service and Prevention Services of Ionia County Community Mental Health, with support from Prevention on the state level.

The decision to provide stress management workshops for female public assistance recipients followed from the finding that the largest group of mental health services consumers in Ionia County in 1975-76 consisted of young, low income women. They presented at the Mental Health Center with a variety of concerns, but marital and family problems were most often noted.

When this information was made available to us, we were generally aware of the fact that people with less money tend to have more problems, and we were interested in the research showing that women who don't work outside the home and who care for children under the age of six are at extremely high risk for becoming clinically depressed.

We knew from working with mental health center clients, that being a poor, young woman with small children, and no one to count

Presented at the DMH Women's Task Force Public Forum, "Life Stages and Stressful Life Events—Marriage and Separation," Grand Rapids, Michigan, December 12, 1980.

Whatever Debbie Marciniak knows of the lives of poor women and how to be of use to them, she learned while working as a VISTA welfare paralegal in a legal aid bureau, a drug counselor in a methadone maintenance program, an outreach therapist in a child abuse and neglect prevention program, and a psychoeducational group leader in a rural community mental health setting.

163

on for emotional or practical support, is not exactly a set-up for mental wellness. We also personally believed that women are generally ill-prepared to take control of their own lives due to traditional societal sex-role conditioning. Learned helplessness theory and stress theory helped us conceptualize what we wanted to do with all of this, as we planned our intervention.

The Stress Management Workshop is intended to help women increase self-esteem, improve interpersonal relationships, develop additional social supports, add to the number of stress management strategies available to them, and begin to believe they are capable of taking control of their lives.

This is how we operate: basic family service workers at the Department of Social Services refer public assistance recipients whom they believe to be at risk for the development of stress-related problems, but who are not exhibiting severe symptoms. We then make home visits to explain the project, including the research component, and to determine the need for child care and transportation (which is provided by the Volunteer Services Bureau at Social Services). The referred individual eventually becomes part of a group of eight to fourteen women, including two facilitators, that meet three hours a week, for ten consecutive weeks at a church in downtown Ionia. The facilitators pitch ideas, and the women are asked to relate to them in terms of their own experiences and situations. Brief written exercises are used to trigger discussion. We rely heavily on the use of visual aids; we make charts and diagrams of everything, attempting to make our ideas as clear as possible.

The workshop is divided into three units: (1) self-esteem; (2) decision-making and life planning; and (3) stress management strategies (with emphasis on how to control what you can and how to cope when your control is severely limited or you are taking a risk and you are scared). Diane Johnson and Roberta Rodgers, who originated the project, felt that in order to teach a woman how to better deal with stress, she first had to believe that she *mattered,* and that she had the power to take charge of her life, thus the heavy emphasis on self-esteem and life planning skills.

My suggestions for people who work with low income women in the mental health system are very simple:

1. *PROVIDE CHILD CARE AND TRANSPORTATION*

It is unrealistic to think that if a woman *really* needs mental health services she will go to the center by hook or by crook. It is just not true. Offering child care and transportation is important not only because women need it, but because it is a way to engage them—they then have two less reasons to say, "Leave me alone, it isn't worth it."

The best transportation arrangement we have found is to reimburse group members who have cars for transporting women who don't. That way, the women have the travel time to develop relationships that begin in group.

2. *DO OUT-REACH AND BE NICE*

Make a home visit to do the intake if at all possible. Let the woman see that you are a nice person who is concerned about her. Let her know what to expect and provide encouragement and reassurance if necessary. While you are there, take a good look around and get a feeling for her reality. (I think all therapists, or at least middle class therapists such as myself, should be required to do periodic home visits. It is too easy to forget what poverty really means; we need to be continually reminded.)

3. *PROVIDE EDUCATIONAL EXPERIENCES AS OPPOSED TO THERAPY*

Although many of the women in our workshops have hit every human services agency in town, and don't balk at the idea of mental health "treatment," there are others who come to our group but would never consider going to the mental health center because of the stigma. (Everyone knows that only crazy people go to Mental Health.)

Issues that always surface in group which could provide the material for additional "educational experiences" are "parenting," "making it on my own," "divorce and custody," "death," "my husband/boyfriend won't talk to me" and "I'm a big nothing" (low self-esteem).

4. *BRING THE WOMEN TOGETHER IN GROUPS*

I feel very strongly that women must have contact with other women. They need opportunities to connect with each other, to see how their problems are related to societal roles. In individual therapy, I believe it is almost impossible for the woman to avoid thinking, "Here we are—you, the "got-it-all-together" therapist and me, the "screwed-up, bad person." In a group you can save time by minimizing that tendency. It is much easier to show that we are all okay. Things happen so much more quickly in group; I get a much greater sense that movement is occurring there than I ever got working with women individually.

5. *SELECT GROUP LEADERS WHO LIKE WOMEN AS PEO-*

PLE, AND WHO AREN'T AFRAID TO BE GROUP MEMBERS THEMSELVES (and if they are or ever were wives and mothers, it is even better)

I believe the group leaders must be willing to be group members, to show their own struggles, to talk about their own efforts to deal with stress-related problems. Most of the women in the workshop groups are absolutely convinced that they are basically different from the facilitators. They believe everyone who is not on welfare has it "all-together" and floats through life without pain or problems.

They love to hear that doctors, lawyers, psychologists and teachers are not immune from emotional problems, pregnant teenage children, dirty custody battles and psychotic episodes. They are entitled to this information.

To discover that they are not essentially different from other people sparks great hope. I feel that a leader who believes she is essentially different from low income women is going to have a hard time with groups like ours, and is likely to be less helpful than one who feels connected in the ways that really matter.

I also think that a good sense of humor should be a requirement for group leaders. The women are so warm and funny themselves, it doesn't seem fair to stick them with someone who can't laugh at herself.

6. *TEACH WOMEN HOW TO MAKE USE OF SUPPORT SOURCES AND ADVOCATE FOR THEM AS YOU DEAL WITH OTHER AGENCIES AND INSTITUTIONS*

Telling a woman that "financial aid to return to school may be available, so check with the community college admissions office," is not enough for women. They need concrete information, they need help to interpret applications, they need to talk to other women who went back to school and were scared too. We have found it is useful to hook women up with each other, even if they were not in the same workshop group, so the one who "did it" can guide the one who is just getting started. Women need to know how to track down information on schools, training programs, jobs, other agencies, etc. They need to know how to get started and what to do when they hit obstacles.

Here I want to share some of the comments made by the women themselves, which are probably more relevant than anything I have to say. We always ask workshop participants what they liked best about the workshop when we do the follow-up, about five months after the workshops end. Here are the seven recurring themes which we have extracted from their responses along with some sample quotes.

"What mattered to me was:

1. *Discovering that other people's problems were as bad or worse than mine.* (This is what they *all* say.)

"Being with other women and learning I wasn't the only one who had problems." "Finding out I'm not a freak after all." "Finding out I wasn't by myself—others have hang-ups." "I'm not always happy now and I do still have minor problems, as everyone does, but I'm about an eight or nine on a ladder of ten . . . that was a big jump from two or three in the beginning."

2. *Having people listen to my ideas and feelings.*

"Being able to talk over problems." "I got to talk about myself which helped a lot." "I can deal better with my problems because of the support I received from other people." "Getting a chance to air and find workable solutions." "It was a time for everyone to be themselves." (We hear this all the time.)

3. *Realizing that I'm okay.*

"I am spending some time on *myself* for a change." "Learning I'm okay." "It helped me feel better about myself and my life." "I have a more positive attitude." "Gaining self-confidence—I can step out more freely." "I am more realistic. I accept me and others more easily." "Made me realize I've accomplished a lot in my life." "Feeling good about myself changing roles." "I can say exactly how I feel and what I think about things. I don't worry whether they think I'm right or not." "I count!!!"

4. *Learning I am capable of taking control of my own life.*

"It's okay to look at the past and then let go of it." "To live one day at a time." "To set goals, planning for the future and not the outcome." "I'm taking control of my life, I'm getting out more." "I don't feel so sorry for myself." "I have taken more charge of my life—started school, found a ride, found a babysitter, not nervous about asking for help anymore, making more friends, more patient with the kids." "I learned to cope with problems and relax when I am under stress." "Can make decisions better on my own." "I learned not to be so shy and I got my husband to talk our problems out instead of yelling and throwing things as I did before." "I went to work and then decided to go to college." "I'm going to school." "Marital relationship is better." "I don't scream at my kids as much as I did before."

5. *Experiencing the open, honest, accepting attitude of the group.*

"The friendliness felt, sharing and caring." "I don't feel the world is against me anymore." "People showed me that they do care about what happens to ya." "The people were friendly—friendly environment." "The honesty and sincerity." "The openness—I was really able to lay my cards on the table."

6. *Getting out of the house and meeting new people.*

"I like being with people." "It was something for me to look forward to each week." "I made new friends." "It gave me a chance to get away from my kids." "I just liked it because I met new people."

7. *Stepping back and looking at my life from a new perspective and understanding better why people act the way they do.*

"Doing the thinking and writing exercises." "The work made me look at myself." "We had to face ourselves and others and came out the better for it." "It made me think and it provided useful information." "It made me think more about my life."

In their evaluations, then, the women continually remind us that being heard, accepted and cared about, helps them to feel better about themselves and enables them to deal more effectively with their problems.

In summary, I believe the best way to see that women are heard, accepted and cared about, is to bring them together and to accept the fact that we may have to go out of our way in order to do so. We may have to concern ourselves with things about which mental health workers don't generally concern themselves—things like child care and transportation and home visits and "back-door" approaches and worrying about how, as individual therapists, we really feel about low income women and their problems.

A Community College Approach to Meeting the Needs of Women

Mary Laing

BACKGROUND INFORMATION ABOUT THE WOMEN'S RESOURCE CENTER

The Women's Resource Center is a service center for people at Lansing Community College and in the surrounding area who may be needing support in life-transition periods, looking for new directions, seeking an understanding of changing roles, developing personal or professional growth skills, exploring career options, or considering return to school.

We offer assistance in these areas through a two-pronged educational approach: a wide range of Student Development class offerings and services which include an opportunity for individuals to discuss concerns with our staff, a community outreach program, and ongoing scholarship and child care/financial aid programs. Special services and scholarships for displaced homemakers are available through the Center. While men are also seen at the Center, a majority of the individuals served are women and the focus here will be on their needs. Most are non-students when we first see them, but many subsequently become students at the community college.

Not all women who come to the Women's Resource Center are poor—but most are needy in that their mental health and functioning are presented as important concerns. In some ways, their needs are the same whether they are poor or not; in other ways their needs are different.

Presented at the Michigan DMH Women's Task Force Public Forum, "An Overview of Women's Mental Health Problems," Lansing, Michigan, September 19, 1980.

Mary Laing is Program Director of the Women's Resource Center at Lansing Community College, Lansing, Michigan.

169

If we describe mental health in the broadest sense, as the optimum functioning of an individual, then our center would be involved primarily in activities that would promote good mental health and assist in preventing or alleviating disabilities.

Here are some examples of problems brought to us by our clientele which are related to their state of mental health.

1. "My husband has left me to go and live with another woman. I have no money and I don't even know how to go about getting a job or even know what kind of work I can do."
2. "My husband died recently. I know I need to find a job, but who will hire me at my age?"
3. "I'd like to go to school, but I don't have the money to pay for my courses."
4. "I'm on ADC (Aid to Dependent Children) and I can't find anyone to take care of my kids while I go to school."
5. "I'm afraid—I just want to go back home. If he comes home and finds out I've been here, he'll beat me again."
6. "Do you know of any way I can get the money for an abortion? I'm not on Medicaid and, as a student, I don't have the money to pay for it."
7. "Is it illegal for a man to tell me during an interview that they need a man for the job because it requires night work?"
8. "The situation was so bad at home that I just left and now I might lose my kids because I left them with my husband. I couldn't take the kids with me because who will take me and the three kids in?"
9. "I have a wide range of experiences, but no formal educational training. My husband always preferred that I not go to school or work so I'd be free to travel with him and entertain his clients. Now that he is gone, I don't know how I'm going to support myself."
10. "I don't really need to work, but I need something to do with my time—something meaningful and interesting."
11. "I'm afraid I'm going to lose my job. My boss has really been pressuring me to go out with him and implying he can help me to advance on the job."
12. "Can you recommend a good doctor (or lawyer) who won't treat me like I'm empty headed?"

These are actual situations and were selected to point out the variety of our clientele. As a part of an educational institution, we cannot begin to provide all the services available elsewhere in the community. Therefore, it is not uncommon for our staff to refer individuals to more appropriate community agencies (other agencies also refer women to us when we are the logical service provider).

The largest number of women we serve are going through some sort of transition in their lives. Often this involves going through a divorce and as a result, having to change their roles (i.e., having to enter the labor market with no recent work experience, lacking skills or having skills that are outdated). Very often the feelings expressed include an overwhelming lack of self-confidence. It is not unusual for these women to exhibit signs of depression, fear, hopelessness, despair and anger. In some instances, this stressful psychological state is accompanied by some physical concerns such as heart problems, back problems, poor diet, and, on occasion, substantial health problems of other family members.

Very often the economic needs of these women add a great deal of stress to their lives at an already difficult time. Having to re-enter the job market with limited skills at a time when our economy is poor, and they lack reliable transportation, or are faced with losing the home they have had for several years, or are trying to locate hard-to-find low cost housing, or are realizing that child care costs will take a substantial amount of their earnings each month. These things in combination become overwhelming and a tremendous burden. We have read often enough that even if they are employed, full-time women workers earn an average of 59¢ for every dollar a man earns. Add to all these concerns raising children as a single parent and you see a very difficult world for many women. (A more universal difficulty is the problem of living in a world which treats women very differently than it does men.) The magnitude and duration of these problems translate into emotional states. Most have a cluster of problems rather than one problem alone. How they feel about and deal with the problems impacts upon their own mental health. The fact that they have come to our Center indicates a positive step in terms of attempting to make some changes in their lives. Our Center is not always the first place our clients have sought help—nor is it always the last.

We have all heard negative stories of treatment clients have received from agencies which are supposed to help them. In some cases, my own efforts to obtain information on behalf of clients have been frustrating.

RECOMMENDATIONS

As service providers, we need to educate ourselves and to examine our own attitudes with respect to women and women's roles and make sure we are sensitive to their needs. We have a responsibility to sensitize others who are working with women in these capacities. We talk about a client's problems, but we have to look at our clients in terms of how they feel about their roles and about their expectations. Many of them need to deal with roles that they have never had to deal with before, and these changes compound their problems.

Some women may not have had any previous financial responsibilities for the family. They might never have ever taken their car in for servicing; they might not know how to change a fuse, or change a filter in the furnace. While their problems taken individually might seem small, when faced with a number of other problems, one or two more of these small problems can have a great deal of impact on a person during times of severe stress.

We need to work with physicians regarding some remaining stereotypic attitudes about women and their presenting problems. Basically, these attitudes tend to result in low levels of service to women, which is sometimes dangerous and is never acceptable. We have to caution professionals to guard against making a diagnosis based simply upon role expectations of a woman client or patient. We still hear terms like "hysterical woman," "hypochondriacal woman," "she's going through the change of life," etc. These terms are used as a diagnosis or an excuse, when in fact, problems may not be rooted in these stereotypic labels. Behaviors may be explained away as "mental health concerns," or dismissed as nothing to worry about, chronic complaining, or failure to adjust to a certain facet of life.

Ideally, I would like to see preventive mental health programs set up, beginning at grade school level. I realize that funding may be a problem, but it is a matter of deciding what is important. We need to encourage young girls at an early age in their endeavors. We need to let them know they are whole people—that they are not something less than boys.

We need to think about special kinds of services to the aging. Most of our older population are females and this number is growing every year. Most of the poor in our country are women, and many of them are older women. Some of our elderly citizens are overly medicated, leading practitioners to mistakenly diagnose mental health problems. Another recommendation from the perspective of our clients and the Center is to expand the dissemination of information about mental health services available in a community. Are the people we really want to reach aware of the services available in their communities? If not, why are they not aware?

How many of us have seen information about services related to mental health care in locations as accessible as laundromats, grocery stores, bus stops, doctors' offices, community centers, day care centers, low cost housing complexes? I raise this question because I believe most of us as providers can improve our dissemination of information and reach the people we may not have reached previously through conventional means.

We need to make sure that whatever information we do disseminate in written form is understandable so that people comprehend what and where the services are and how to access those services. We want to make sure that our publications are bilingual, so that we don't exclude a part of our population who might have some difficulty with English.

My last recommendation is to encourage a comprehensive and well-coordinated system of service delivery so that groups of women do not lose out due to gaps in services. The end result of good coordination is good service delivery to clients. As a side effect, we may also cut costs for agencies providing these services by ensuring that dollars are spent on services which are most needed and by keeping duplication of services to a minimum.

In summary, mental health-related care providers should take women and their problems seriously. Stereotypic attitudes have no place in the mental health system. We who care about women need to take the initiative. We need to sensitize and train those who are working as mental health providers. We need to improve means of getting and disseminating information to prospective users and we need to better coordinate available services.

A person who is discriminated against in any society cannot enjoy the same quality of mental health as those against whom society does not discriminate. Discriminatory practice impacts heavily, and negatively, upon the mental health of women. While this problem of discrimination is much larger than what we can expect to change through just these few efforts, at the very least our awareness of its impact can have some effect on our own practices.

Summary and Recommendations: Advancing Innovative Mental Health Programs for Women

> What mattered to me was being with other women and learning I wasn't the only one who had problems.
>
> Participant in a Stress Management
> Workshop for Low-Income Women,
> from Marciniak (1980)

> It is clear that the emotional problems of low-income mothers cannot be solved by mental health professionals alone. Low-income mothers need access to jobs which will support their families above the poverty line. They need child care options which will provide trustworthy care for their children. Many women also need access to forms of mutual support and therapy which take into account the social origins of depression and its roots in discrimination, poverty and overwhelming responsibilities.
>
> Belle et al. (1980)

It has been established through many sources that women are over-represented as clients of mental health services. Despite this over-representation, women have not necessarily benefited from the services they receive. The Women's Task Force found substantial evidence that mental health services are not meeting many women's needs. Furthermore, there are considerable numbers of women who are inappropriately utilizing mental health services or incorrectly defining themselves as having mental health problems. We have concluded that some women may be better served as "non-clients" by diverting many who now utilize mental health services into support groups. Such

175

groups have been found to be especially helpful to women experiencing stressful life events (i.e., aging, raising of a handicapped or chronically ill child, pregnancy, divorce, etc.). The number of women now experiencing these and other acute or chronically stressful life situations is alarming. The Women's Task Force is convinced that a change of focus in the current treatment of these groups of women is in order.

At this point in time over one half of all women work and 46 percent of these working women have children at home. In fact, only 14 percent of all American families now fit into the stereotypical "father at work," "mother at home" pattern (Rohrbaugh, 1979). "Uncoupling," whether as a result of divorce, separation, or death of a spouse, is a reality for many women who had previously found their identity through marriage and family. It is no surprise, then, that many women are experiencing stressful life events and so find themselves at risk for loss of identity and self-confidence.

Very often, a woman's economic needs add a great deal of stress to her life at an already difficult time. For many women, especially those we categorize as displaced housewives, a change of marital status leaves little choice but to look for employment (for many, after years of absence from the work force). And it is well established that women are disadvantaged in the work force, receiving 59¢ for every dollar their male counterparts earn. Minority women often bear a double burden by being disadvantaged both by race and gender.

Likewise, there are a number of stressful life events that women may experience more frequently and/or intensively than men; among them: crises of childbirth (including teen pregnancy and abortion), single parenting, isolation/displacement from the homemaker role, domestic abuse, and victimization. A myriad of women are overwhelmed by the disruption these events place on their lives and are facing the task of developing new role definitions and expectations. And since women are more often responsible for the care of children, the combining of nurturant and occupational roles (especially when concurrent with a difficult life event) often results in role confusion, stress and coping problems. For some women (especially single mothers), the striving for emotional and economic independence involves the expectation of becoming a superwoman by being all things to all people. The role overload often resulting from this situation has a definite impact on women's mental health. Because women tend to blame themselves rather than recognizing the inherently stressful nature of their situations, many women under stress will see themselves as ''crazy'' and seek out professional mental health services. What these women need is support and guidance while coping with many of these difficult transitions—*not* a mental health professional.

In other cases, because of the stigma attached to receiving mental health services, many women inwardly label themselves but continue to try to make it on their own without support. For these women a whole array of services are needed (but are often unavailable) to help them cope with their acute or chronically stressful life events. Continued and unabated stress can be a major factor in producing mental and physical health disease, damage or breakdown. Thus, for many of these women, problems exacerbate to the point of dysfunction. They then enter the mental health system, remain there for long periods of time, are labeled as ''ill,'' and placed in a position of dependency on a system that is still operating under assumptions about women's roles that are antiquated and in great need of revision.

The Women's Task Force has concluded that it would be more beneficial to divert a large portion of the women who are now being served on a one-to-one basis into support groups. For many women, severe mental health problems could have been avoided if support services had been available *before* their stressful situations produced extreme results.

The Women's Task Force has received testimony and documentation that support groups can and do work. Self-help/support groups are no longer a faddish movement. Evidence has accumulated that, for many, they are at least as effective as traditional one-on-one interventions:

While self-help/mutual aid groups for a variety of afflictions have been on the scene for nearly 50 years, recent research reveals that they represent a growing and significant resource for helping vast segments of society. (Borman, 1981)

Through participation in support groups, many women share common problems and provide each other with mutual aid, thereby developing new social support systems. In addition, support groups provide not only emotional support but education as well. Furthermore, this synthesis of support and education has a direct relationship to problem-solving.

There are many examples of support groups with demonstrated effectiveness. For instance, the stress management program utilizes an intervention approach combining group support and training to help women increase self-esteem, improve interpersonal relationships, develop additional social supports and provide new strategies for managing stress. Women in the program are able to feel better about themselves, deal more effectively with their problems and develop the sense of competence needed to assume better control of their lives.

Other noteworthy support group approaches have included a Woman's Resource Center group for incest victims, a widow to widow group, divorce adjustment, women in transition, incest family treatment, and many outstanding others.

A movement away from traditional mental health services into self-help/support groups would not only produce effective outcomes but would also eliminate a great deal of the stigma associated with utilization of mental health services, and would also ultimately cost less than serving these same women individually. Non-traditional treatment approaches and locations are viable solutions to the labeling phenomenon so prevalent in mental health settings today; and by diverting women into support groups, the problem of the stigma attached to absorption into the mental health system is ameliorated.

Problems of fear and stigma in seeking help are especially pertinent to women who are victims of domestic abuse. Exposure through contact with a professional agency can be a trigger to a violent male whose victim is usually well aware that survival depends on keeping her abuse a secret from "the authorities" and government services. Fear of the stigma attached to mental health service utilization is also a major concern for women residing in rural areas where anonymity is difficult to maintain.

Cost-reductions could also occur through greater use of support groups. Individuals themselves can become the providers of services and help, as well as the consumers. Victims' experiences can become resources to others.

The Women's Task Force has determined that a new approach is needed for women experiencing stressful life events. Therefore, the Task Force recommends that more support groups need to be established in non-traditional, non-threatening settings (i.e., churches, schools, neighborhood centers, etc.).

The role of the mental health professional must change to facilitate implementation of this approach. Mental health professionals will be called upon to exercise more consultation and education activities on a community level. A portion of those energies now invested in the traditional one-on-one mode of treatment may be more effectively used in increased program and case consultation. The end result of this shift to increased group participation will mean that more clients will be served, using the same mental health resources.

Other new options for alternative treatment must be employed, especially those which focus less on pathology and more on the individual's healthy functioning side. There are some outstanding examples of non-traditional programs, such as the Elizabeth Stone House, which provide alternatives for women who are in distress due to pressures and life event crises. Non-sexist therapy is another non-traditional approach to the treatment of women that has developed from a growing understanding of the relationship between the socialization of women and their mental health problems. Its intended outcome is to help women achieve their own emotional and human potential. Such programs and treatment approaches should be given continued support by professionals and administrators in the public mental health system.

It is also essential that a sound referral network be established and maintained between community mental health agencies and programs which address women's problems (i.e., shelters for battered women). Community mental health must not only be aware of other resources available to their female clients, but furthermore, should make an all-out effort to contribute to the support and development (including staff training) of innovative programs for women in their community.

Women need opportunities to connect with each other, to acknowledge the universality of their dilemmas and joys. Women need the opportunity to talk to other women as a group and realize that they are not alone; that their problems and reactions don't make them "crazy." Too often in the past, public education has been something that service programs had little time for. Sharing a common experience often does more to expedite progress in problem resolution than many other types of interventions.

Participation in support groups can be very efficacious for women in adapting to life stresses and changes without making them mental health clients. The mental health system must provide the encouragement, resources, and staffing to make these groups a reality.

RECOMMENDATIONS

A. Direct Services

1. The public mental health system should have adequately trained staff on call to respond to mental health needs presented by women victims of violence in emergency rooms, rape centers and shelter programs.

B. Indirect Services

1. Much of the existing service delivery to women and the community mental health caseload should be analyzed to determine the extent to which individuals served have problems in living which require education and support vs. problems which require the

intervention of a mental health professional. Based on such analysis, major changes in mental health programs from individual therapy to support groups should be made.

2. To help women deal with mental health problems before they become more serious and cause them to become clients, public mental health agencies should serve as an information and referral source or, if necessary, initiator of support groups for women, especially focusing on women's life stages and stressful life events. Mental health agencies should take a leadership role in forming and organizing such groups (where none exist) by offering consultation, public relations efforts, resources and supplies, training to group leaders, etc. An especially helpful model in such support groups is for agency staff persons to train volunteers who can then work to help other women.

3. Alternative services in the community, such as support groups, should be offered that do not require women to become clients or patients of the mental health system—e.g., services offered at the churches, the YWCA and other non-clinical, non-sick locations. This is especially important for minority women, because of the even greater problems of stigmatization which they experience.

4. Mental health agencies should circulate and distribute contact and referral information on support groups for women to locations where target group members are most likely to see it.

5. As state mental health agencies move out of direct service delivery, they should assume a greater role in public education and consciousness-raising. This is especially important concerning women's mental health issues because there is so much misinformation.

6. Community mental health should work with other community groups to focus on sexual harassment and victimization of women as important community issues.

7. Community mental health, in conjunction with com-

munity agencies, should sponsor life-planning and career-planning for women to help them see their lives as a continuum extending into the future rather than jumping from life event to life event.

8. Assertiveness training is critical for women since they are often taught to be passive and listen to authority. They need to learn that they can help themselves. The mental health system should support this at national, state, and local levels.

9. Mental health agencies should work with educational programs to provide policy advice as to how they could improve the mental health of women and create a positive image for girls that they are important in their own right.

10. Community mental health should work with local libraries and community groups to help put on community outreach programs, what it means to be a woman, women's problems, etc.

11. Community mental health services should help initiate educational and support groups for first-time parents, starting with pregnancy, childbirth and early child development. These could be carried out through schools, PTA, YMCA, church groups, etc.

12. The mental health system should work with educational and medical institutions to produce information which helps women understand the emotional reactions which may occur as a normal result of hormonal changes.

C. Administration of Mental Health Services

1. State and federal mental health agencies should develop a better incentive system to promote the use of non-traditional services and/or consultation and education services so that agencies are encouraged to treat individuals more effectively, in groups, for shorter times and/or avoid conferring the label of client unless necessary.

2. Due to a reduction of public funds, the mental health system must identify and disseminate specific models of providing services to a larger, less disturbed group,

who, with some assistance from the local mental health center, could lead a more productive life for themselves and their children.

3. The mental health system should develop informational material for women who want to volunteer to get involved with women's mental health support services: Where to go? Who to see: What to do? This should be written in a way that promotes public media distribution.

4. Through support of demonstration projects, the mental health system should:

   a. establish non-traditional alternatives to inpatient treatment for women, where women can find rehabilitation and the meaning of their experience and avoid the stigma of institutionalization.

   b. explore innovative ways of meeting the mental health needs of rural women, to offset service inaccessibility created by large geographical distances.

   c. identify innovative models for service delivery for chronically mentally ill women who are returned to their communities.

   d. make funds available for working with and treating identified groups of black women, especially in urban areas, utilizing innovative modalities.

5. The mental health system must support scientific evaluations of small programs which represent a substantial change from the usual women's treatment regime, e.g., COPE, Widow-to-Widow programs, Elizabeth Stone House, etc.

D. Continuing Education/Inservice Training

1. Curriculum and training materials on working with community/caregiver agencies for community mental health administrators and direct care staff should be developed to assist in a shift from traditional one-on-one outpatient therapy interventions to a role of development, utilization, consultation and training for support groups for women, based in community agencies.

E. Training for Mental Health Professionals

1. University training programs for mental health professionals should provide appropriate coursework and field experiences that include communication and consultation with other agencies regarding programs or cases. In addition, it is essential that students acquire a better understanding of community systems. This aspect of professional training must be an integral part of all programs.

F. Public Policy Support

1. Since standard health insurance does not pay for help given in support groups, ways should be investigated to provide funding sources for indirect services, e.g., influencing third-party reimbursers to pay for these services.
2. The public mental health system at state and local levels should serve to communicate information to the public about women's mental health problems: a recognition of the social, family and economic stresses women are under and the fact that such stresses and the social bias and discrimination that women are subjected to are reasons for women's anger.
3. To better understand women and the effects of critical life stages, resource material should be packaged that covers topics such as menstruation, pregnancy, menopause, marriage, aging, etc., and distributed to self-help groups.
4. The educational system (adult education and community colleges) should recognize the emotional needs (including loneliness, isolation, etc.) of adults who enroll in educational/craft courses by providing social hours or other opportunities for socialization.

SECTION 6:
PREVENTION OF MENTAL HEALTH PROBLEMS FOR WOMEN IN THE WORK PLACE

ON A WOMAN'S PLACE . . . . .

Shall the home be our world. . .or the world our home.

Charlotte Perkins Gilman
(Reeves, 1973)

ON WOMEN AND WORK . . . . .

The "average woman" is a statistical creation, a fiction. She has been used to defend the status quo of the labor market, on the assumption that knowing the sex of an employee reliably predicts his or her job attitudes. This assumption is false. Knowing that a worker is female allows us to predict that she will hold a job in a "woman's field," and that she will be substantially underpaid for a person of her qualifications. But knowing that a worker is female does not help us much to predict what she wants from her job.

Crowley et al. (1973)

ON SOCIAL CHANGE . . . . .

Social change itself can be a source of stress, particularly when institutions are slow to recognize such change when it occurs. For example, society's failure

185

to provide adequate child care services is a major contributor to the role overload of women.

Russo and VandenBos (1980)

INTRODUCTION

The preceding sections have focused on women with mental health problems: What are the problems? How do they differ from men's? What are the barriers to women receiving appropriate treatment? What are some innovative treatment alternatives that might better serve women with mental health problems? This section is an effort to move backward—to a point in time *before* these women had problems—examining the stress women experience from the dual role many of them play: as worker and as homemaker. Since the mental health system is composed primarily of females in its work force, we would urge mental health service agencies to place a primary emphasis on preventing mental health problems in their women workers. Such an approach would serve to improve the effectiveness of the services provided (by ensuring energized and more motivated workers) and also to prevent some mental health workers from becoming future mental health clients (by decreasing stress which can often cause mental health problems).

THE PROBLEMS

Since the turn of the century, women have been entering and exiting the work force, demonstrating their flexibility and willingness to function where and when they were needed. This was especially evident during periods of international conflict. In the 1950s and 1960s, it was assumed that women were entering the work force to supplement their husbands' salaries, to earn ''pin money'' for those exciting new consumables that our society was churning out. Some decided to work long enough to help meet the rising costs of college tuitions.

But then things changed. As a result of rising inflation, rising divorce rates, and an increase in the absolute numbers of female-headed households, women no longer could afford *not* to work. What had been considered a deviant role for women years ago, has become an often necessary woman's role today—that is, the role of provider. But, the changes described have not necessarily benefited women. A recent national survey found that the group registering a considerable increase in reports of job unhappiness from 1957 to 1976 were women (Veroff et al., 1981). At the same time, work commitment has increased for women and is now almost as high as men's. Furthermore, along with these changes in work and family roles, the growth of families headed by women is astounding. Although these families constitute one-seventh of the total number of families in the United States, they include one-half of all families living in poverty (Russo and VandenBos, 1980). And minority women are overrepresented as heads of such households. Add to this the fact that low-income mothers with young children have the highest rate of depression of any demographic group (Belle, 1980), and the full scope of the problem intensifies.

Many of these women are entering the job market with limited skills at a time when the overall state of our economy is generally poor. Large numbers lack dependable transportation and are searching to find decent, low cost housing; at the same time, they face the realization that the cost of child care alone will consume a substantial amount of their earnings each month. Concerns about raising children as a single parent compound these others, and eventually female heads of households must face a cluster of problems rather than a single issue.

Regardless of marital status, mothers seeking work face a tremendous shortage of part-time job opportunities. And as things now stand, women have more responsibility for their children's care. They still do the bulk of the housework and child care, even when employed full-time. Veroff et al. (1981) found that 80% of male and female respondents in their national survey perceived that women do most of the housework, whether or not they work. Women need relief to actively participate in their jobs. They need assurance that their children's needs are being met in their absence. Many women experience a great deal of stress in trying to compromise between home and work. This stress is very likely to have an impact on the mental health of women workers and their families. Women need options open to them in the work place so that they can be free to explore and develop their potential and maintain their mental well-being without jeopardizing their future economic security.

TREATMENT OF WOMEN AT THE WORK PLACE

The public mental health system should adopt work arrangements that are supportive, not detrimental, to women and the problems and stresses they face when balancing family and work. It should act as a role model by providing options in scheduling to women workers, such as job sharing and flexible time. In addition, there should be more sensitivity to family needs through provision or support of adequate child care arrangements. The need for good child care programs has been justified in the past in terms of developing the child's potential; but without affordable and quality child care arrangements, many mothers (especially single mothers) may not be able to work or may be forced to use less than adequate arrangements, adding to their own stress and guilt. Child care should also be available to women who *do not* work to allow them some respite from family responsibilities; this can also contribute to the well-being of the whole family.

Not only should women be free to work, but women must be able to obtain jobs and careers of their choice. Contributing to many of the previously mentioned women's work issues is the fact that women are blatantly absent from positions of authority or decision-making in all facets of the work force. Realistically, there is little promise of women's employment situation changing until women gain equal access to higher status positions in business, government, and human service agencies. To ameliorate this imbalance, people in administrative positions must be motivated to initiate changes. But how many women now hold administrative positions? Or perhaps more succinctly, how supportive are men in these positions of changing inequities? It logically follows that until more women assume administrative positions, little will change. For instance, it is known that only 2% of all corporate board directorships are held by women (U.S. Department of Labor, 1981). This statistic certainly exemplifies the gravity of the inequities found in the work force. Indeed, there are myriad possibilities of insidious ways that business and agencies avoid promoting women; but a portion of the responsibility must fall upon the shoulders of women themselves. Unless more women gain confidence in their abilities and therefore take the initiative to apply to these desired positions, few changes will occur.

Many of the inequities women experience in their jobs and careers were brought to the attention of the Women's Task Force. For instance, in Michigan, there is a disparity in educational requirements, legal responsibility, and scope of practice between Clinical Nurse Specialists and Physician's Assistants. Although the Clinical Nurse Specialist has more training and more autonomy in working with patients, she is consistently paid less.*

SUPPORTING WORKING PARENTS AND FAMILIES

Just as women are socialized to assume a greater portion of the caring for others, men are socialized to assume the occupational role and are expected to have more distant-type relationships with their children—being only marginally involved in matters of their daily care. However, it should be noted that some males have begun to express the opinion that the "distant father" stereotype works equally to the detriment of fathers as well as mothers. They feel that fathers have missed out on much of the positive experiences of child development.

---

*In Michigan, the requirements for a Clinical Nurse Specialist are a Baccalaureate degree in Nursing plus 18-24 months in a clinical area of practice. Whereas, the requirements for a Physician's Assistant (P.A.) are two years in a community college plus two years of a liberal arts background. P.A.'s trained in other states and practicing in Michigan have completed educational requirements ranging from six months to one year.

Recent studies (Biller, 1974) have demonstrated the important role fathers play in early phases of family development. One study (Hersh and Levin, 1978) showed significantly stronger bonding between fathers and infants when the fathers were involved with their babies in the first three days after childbirth. Furthermore, fathers have been excluded from other aspects of responsibility for their children such as in traditional therapeutic interventions. Research on successful outcomes of therapeutic treatment of children (Wolper, 1980) supports the interpretation that the more the father is involved in treatment, the greater the likelihood of success for the child. The public mental health system should encourage men to have equal and active participation in their families by urging fathers' involvement in family therapy. It would be beneficial to all family members for fathers to have a greater acceptance, encouragement and participation in shared childbirth experiences and in child caring.

Likewise, the public mental health system could act as a role model for other agencies by establishing new policies for men, such as paternity leave, that would enable fathers to share both responsibility and power in their families. By increasing fathers' involvement in the family, the burdens and role overload experienced by many mothers can be substantially lessened, and the end result may well have a definite impact on women's mental health.

RECOMMENDATIONS

To effect these desirable changes involving treatment of women workers and support of working parents and families, the Women's Task Force believes that mental health agencies could become role models and therefore makes the following recommendations:

A. Administration of Mental Health Services

1. Meaningful changes in treatment delivered to women cannot occur unless more women are placed in high level administrative positions in the mental health system. Therefore, the Women's Task Force ada-

mantly recommends that the public mental health system re-evaluate its administrative structure. The Task Force further recommends that the system hasten the process of placing women in decision-making capacities and thereby act as a role model for other employers in human service agencies, business and industry.

2. The mental health system should require equal participation of women in the decision-making process of the system at all levels.

3. The public mental health system should itself provide more flexible work arrangements for women: credit for voluntary work experience in hiring, opportunities for professional women to work part-time or do job sharing to maintain skills and involvement. (Such women might be the most appropriate therapists for women in similar circumstances.) Since mental health agencies employ large numbers of women, they should be ''role models'' for offering child care arrangements which could also be used for training through a linkage to the universities.

4. Top management in mental health agencies should deal with their own sexism, e.g., through awareness training groups.

5. Rights advisors, clients and mental health advocates should be given complete information as to the available remedies for sex discrimination under state and federal laws.

6. Realizing the needs of men and women are interconnected, the mental health system should examine all of its counseling services and procedures to see if men are systematically excluded versus being afforded equal and active participation with their families.

7. Mental health agencies should form women's task forces to provide the women's perspective to policy-level decisions.

8. Mental health agencies should work with high schools to ensure an adequate curriculum in marriage education, family living and parenting, which may help to prevent violence toward women.

9. Supportive mechanisms should be operationalized for

mental health nurses to be primary health care providers practicing within the scope of their license for inpatients and in preventive mental health community programs. Nursing intervention need not necessarily be terminated just because the physician discharges the patient from his or her care. Experimental units in state facilities operated by clinical nurse specialists with physician-support should be encouraged.

B. Continuing Education/Inservice Training

1. Individuals providing counseling to the unemployed should especially be made aware of differences in impacts on men and women.
2. As a continuing education priority, training funds should be provided to nurses in the state mental health facilities so that they will be able to practice nursing instead of functioning primarily as basic caregivers.

C. Public Policy Support

1. Mental health agencies should help put more focus on the stress of working women, the myth of the superwoman and the necessity of men taking on more homemaking responsibilities. This can be done through public statements and work with the media to provide more information on these types of women's problems.
2. The mental health system should support the existence of readily available and flexible quality day-care facilities, especially for single parent heads-of-families working outside the home and also for women or men who need time for themselves and/or for domestic chores.
3. Understanding that the compromise between career and involvement in the home may hold out the best hope for the depressed housewife and single mother, government and private industry should be encouraged to provide more opportunities for job sharing and flexible job hours.

SECTION 7:
CONCLUSIONS

We must do more than simply make our knowledge available to the decision makers of our society. . .We must advocate, assert, urge and proselytize. Each of us must decide how he or she can best contribute to the reduction of the dehumanizing forces in our society and the enhancement of the human competence that is possible. But we must first agree that the problem is in the system, not in the victim!

George W. Albee (1981, p. 27)

Women must convert their ''love'' for and reliance on strength and skill in others to a love for all manner of strength and skill in themselves. . .This requires discipline, courage, confidence, anger, the ability to act, and an overwhelming sense of joy and urgency. . .The centuries of female spiritual, political, and sexual sacrifice will be better redeemed by the female entry into humanity and public institutions than by rejecting them because they are not perfect—or because the efforts to integrate them are difficult and heartbreaking—or because they have traditionally been based on the oppression of women.

Phyllis Chesler (1973, p. 298)

This monograph has presented information on sex differences in the prevalence of mental health problems. We have included in-depth descriptions of diagnoses that are particularly prevalent in women, through research reviews and case studies. These include depression, anorexia nervosa, agoraphobia and hysteria. We have also shown the problems women have in obtaining appropriate treatment; that is, existing treatment approaches may be either male-oriented, sexist, biased, discriminatory or based on out-moded ideas about women. On the other hand, we have also shown several innovative, non-traditional approaches to helping women with mental health problems and the successes which they have demonstrated. Self-help/mutual support groups hold special promise for many types of women's problems—either as an alternative or adjunct to professional therapy. Finally, we have indicated how stresses in the work place and from the combined roles of worker, homemaker and mother may cause eventual mental health problems for women; these stresses may be alleviated through employer-provided options like job sharing, flexible time and child care and through policies which promote the involvement of *both* parents with their families.

We hope that, by now, the reader is convinced of George Albee's conclusion that ''the problem is in the system, not in the victim!'' Over and over again, our material substantiates how women are victimized. Inequities in social status and pervasive sex discrimination can make women feel that they have no control over their outcomes, that they are helpless, and that their self-worth is questionable. Or ultimately, to *think* they are crazy or become *so* depressed that they need a psychiatric label. And women may also be victimized by the mental health service system designed to ''help'' them: treatment which is based on a male model; counseling which upholds the traditional woman's role as the desired outcome of therapy, rejecting non-traditional alternatives even when called for to meet individually-based needs; sexual harassment or exploitation by male therapists; family counseling which urges a wife's submission to her husband's needs and desires, cites the woman's contribution to causing and sustaining spouse abuse, or blames the mother for her children's emotional disturbances.

If you are convinced that the blame must be on the system and not the victim, then you know that certain oft-cited solutions will *not* end the problem as for instance, assertiveness training. While this may provide a useful set of skills to some women to help them improve communication, to feel better about themselves and to avoid being constantly run over, acquiring assertiveness is *not* a panacea to the problems that many women face. A woman who starts being appropriately and persistently assertive about discriminatory pay or lack of comparable worth in male and female salary schedules may find herself out of a job or stereotyped as a ''bitchy, pushy broad'' and worse off than she was before. Individual women acquiring better skills, education, competencies or self-concepts may not be better off if opportunities are still blocked. Indeed, increased frustration, suppressed anger, more anxiety and depression may result.

The answer is action at the larger system level, ''female entry into humanity,'' to quote Chesler. This monograph has described many action answers: treatment alternatives *and* prevention approaches. The Women's Task Force has evolved numerous recommendations for change involving mental health service administration, direct service delivery, continuing education, university training and overall public policy practices. We believe that now, again quoting George Albee, it is up to each of us ''to decide how he or she can contribute'' (Albee, op cit.) and develop strength and skill in ourselves to do it.

And if we, ourselves, are to avoid frustration and depression in attempting system change, we must begin with realistic and feasible, albeit small, goals for change—those aspects of the operation of our programs over which we may have some effect.

In selecting our strategies for change, we must not forget the importance of coalition-building efforts. Women often underestimate the power and significance they can assume when they can coalesce and merge their diverse concerns into a unified force. Jean Baker Miller suggests a coming together of women service providers and women service recipients as a powerful strategy for change. In numbers alone, our strength would be great: women compose the majority of direct care workers and clients in mental health agencies.

As it is now, each group, if they advocate at all, does so for their own special interests: staff for better pay scales,

less contact time and paperwork, or more staff development activities; clients for an end to forced drugging and
involuntary treatment and more consumer-run alternative
services. What if women—staff and patients—united to advocate for changes beneficial to their common interests?
We need more programs/treatment alternatives which are
geared toward *women's* special needs and concerns; many
could be consumer-directed with technical assistance, consultation, facilitators or resources provided by the mental
health agency. We need to provide educational programs
geared to meet staff *and* client needs, like assertiveness
training, stress management and burnout, coping with
depression through positive thinking, or sensitivity to
medicating appropriately and recognizing side effects. We
need staff and clients advocating together for more women
who are feminists on governing boards and in executive
level positions, so that all these changes would be more
likely to occur.

This is not an easy task. Workers and clients have *not*
often worked together or even recognized any common
goals. Workers would have to put aside some of *their* own
biases which emphasize the weaknesses rather than the
strengths of their clients and which assume that the omni-
scient, omnipotent therapist knows what's best for his or
her client. As Kelli Quinn warns (in her chapter in this
monograph), we must avoid replacing patriarchy with
matriarchy. The task will be difficult for clients too: for
some, it will mean putting aside their anger and channeling
it toward more productive outcomes. For others, it will
mean accepting equality with their therapists and consequently, more responsibility for their own treatment and
outcomes.

Building such coalitions will be a long, arduous process,
but it may be one of the few effective ways available to produce the kind of change we are advocating. Human services
funding is not likely to increase; women comprise an increasingly larger percentage of the poverty population. Both
our economic status and support base are falling. The holes
in the safety nets are getting larger and larger. But we *do*
have numbers. And numbers can still make a difference, *if*
we can unite!

Bibliography

Al-Issa, Ihsan. *The Psychopathology of Women.* Englewood Cliffs, New Jersey: Prentice-Hall, 1980.

Albee, G.W. "The Prevention of Sexism." *Professional Psychology* 12 (Feb., 1981): 20-28.

American Psychological Association. "Report of the Task Force on Sex Biases and Sex-Role Stereotyping in Psychotherapeutic Practice." *American Psychologist* 30 (1975): 169-175.

Balter, Mitchell. (Personal Communication) June, 1981.

Beavers, R.W. *Psychotherapy and Growth: A Family Systems Perspective.* New York: Brunner/Mazel, 1977.

Belle, D., and Goldman, N. "Patterns of Diagnoses Received by Men and Women." In *The Mental Health Treatment of Women,* pp. 21-20. Edited by M. Guttentag et al. New York: Academic Press, 1980.

Belle, Deborah et al. *Fighting Stress and Depression: Exemplary Programs for Low-Income Mothers.* Cambridge, Massachusetts: Stress and Families Project, Harvard University, 1980.

Belle, Deborah. (Personal Communication) July, 1982.

Belle, D., ed. *Lives in Stress.* Beverly Hills: Sage Publications, 1982.

Belote, Betsy. *Sexual Intimacy between Female Clients and Male Psychotherapist: Masochistic Sabotage.* PhD Dissertation, California School of Professional Psychology, July 1974.

Bemis, K.M. "Current Approaches to the Etiology and Treatment of Anorexia Nervosa." *Psychological Bulletin* 85 (1978): 593-617.

Bernard J. *The Future of Marriage.* New York: World Publishing Co., 1972.

Bernardez, T. "Women's Groups." In *Handbook of Short-Term Therapy Groups,* pp. 119-138. Edited by M. Rosenbaum. New York: McGraw Hill, 1983.

Bernadez, T. "Women and Anger: Conflicts with Aggression in Contemporary Women." *Journal of the American Medical Women's Association* 33 (1978): 215-219.

Bloom, Bernard L. "Prevention of Mental Disorders: Recent Advances in Theory and Practice." *Community Mental Health Journal* 15 (Fall, 1979): 179-191.

Borman, Leonard D. "Introduction–Helping People to Help Themselves–Self-Help and Prevention." *Prevention in Human Services* 1 (Spring, 1982): 3-15.

Boskind-White, M., and White, W.C. *Bulimorexia: The Binge/Purge Cycle.* New York: W.W. Norton, 1983.

Bosma, B.J. Attitudes of Women Therapists Toward Women Clients, Or a Comparative Study of Feminist Therapy." *Smith College Studies in Social Work* 46 (1975): 53-54.

Breines, W., and Gordon, L. "The New Scholarship on Family Violence." *Signs* 8 (1983): 490-531.

Brodsky, Annette M., and Hare-Mustin, Rachel. *Women and Psychotherapy.* New York: Guilford Press, 1980.

Broverman, I.K., Broverman, D.M., Clarkson, D.E., Rosenkrantz, P.S., and Vogel, S.R. "Sex-Role Stereotypes and Clinical Judgments of Mental Health." *Journal of Consulting and Clinical Psychology* 34 (1970): 1-7.

Brown, G., Bhrolchain, M., and Harns, T. "Social Class and Psychiatric Disturbance Among Women in an Urban Population." *Sociology* 9 (1975): 225-254.

Brown, G.W., and Harris, T. *The Social Origins of Depression: A Study of Psychiatric Disorder in Women.* London: Tavistock, 1978.

Bruch, H. "Anorexia Nervosa and Its Treatment." *Journal of Pediatric Psychology* 2 (1977): 110-12.

Bruch, H. "Anorexia Nervosa." In *Nutrition and the Brain.* Edited by J.J. Wurtman and R.J. Wurtman. New York: Raven Press, 1979.

Cameron, Norma. *Personality and Psychopathology: A Dynamic Approach.* Boston: Houghton Mifflin, 1963.

Canning, H., and Mayer, J. "Obesity–Its Possible Effect on College Acceptance." *New England Journal of Medicine* 275 (1966): 1172-1174.

Carmen, E., Russo, N., and Miller, J. "Inequality and Women's Mental Health: An Overview." *American Journal of Psychiatry* 138 (1981): 1319-1330.

Chesler, Phyllis. *Women and Madness.* New York: Avon Books, 1973.

Chodoff, Paul. "Hysteria and Women." *American Journal of Psychiatry* 139 (1982): 545-551.

Chodorow, N. *The Reproduction of Mothering.* Berkeley: University of California Press, 1978.

Clifford, E. "Body Satisfaction in Adolescence." *Perceptual and Motor Skills* 33(1971): 119-125.

Cooperstock, R. "Psychotropic Drug Use Among Women." *Canadian Medical Association Journal* 115(1976): 760-763.

Corsp, A.H. *Anorexia Nervosa: Let Me Be.* New York: Grune and Stratton, 1980.

Corsp, A.H., Palmer, R.L., and Kalucy, R.S. "How Common is Anorexia Nervosa? A Prevalence Study." *British Journal of Psychiatry* 128 (1976): 549-554.

Costello, C.G. "Social Factors Associated with Depression: A Retrospective Community Study." *Psychological Medicine* 12(1982): 329.

D'Addario, Linda. *Sexual Relationships Between Female Clients and Male Therapists.* PhD Dissertation, California School of Professional Psychology, July 1977.

Dahlberg, C.C. "Sexual Contact Between Patient and Therapist." *Contemporary Psychoanalysts* 6(1970): 107-124.

Dammann, G. "Female Polydrug Abuses: Fact and Fiction." In *Issues on Women and Treatment.* Edited by Ann Bauman. Washington D.C.: National Drug Abuse Council, 1977.

Deming, W.E. "A Recursion Formula for the Proportion of Persons Having a First Admission as Schizophrenic." *Behavioral Science* 13(1968): 467-476.

Dinnerstein, D. *The Mermaid and the Minotaur.* New York: Harper and Row, 1976.

Edelwich, Jerry, and Brodsky, Archi. *Sexual Dilemmas for the Helping Professional.* New York: Brunner/Mazel, 1982.

Eigen, Michael. "The Call and the Lure" *Psychotherapy: Theory, Research and Practice* 10 (Fall, 1973): 194-197.

Engel, G.L. "Conversion Symptoms." In *Signs and Symptoms: Applied Physiology and Clinical Interpretation.* Edited by C.M. MacBryde. Philadelphia: J.B. Lippincott, 1970.

Fabricant, B. "The Psychotherapist and Female Patient: Perceptions and Change." In *Women in Therapy.* Edited by V. Franks and V. Brutle. New York: Brunner/Mazel, 1974.

Fibel, Bobbi. "Transcendence of Sex Roles: Parallel Cultural and Psychotherapeutic Change Process." Paper presented at Symposium on the Process of the Sex Role Integration in Psychotherapy, American Psychological Association, Washington, D.C., 1976.

Fidell, Linda S. "Summary of Psychotropic Drug Usage Among Women" (For President's Commission on Mental Health). Northridge, California: Psychology Department, California State University, 1977.

Fishman, P. "Interaction: The Work Women Do." *Social Problems* 25(1978): 397-406.

Fleming, P.D., Luepker, E.T., Nye, S.G., and Schoener, G. "Treatment Services: Legal Issues for Clients Who Have Been Sexually Involved with Psychotherapists." Presented at the Annual Meeting of the American Orthopsychiatric Association, San Francisco, California, April 2, 1982.

Fodor, I.G. "The Phobic Syndrome in Women." In *Women in Therapy*. Edited by V. Franks, and V. Brutle. New York: Brunner/Mazel, 1974.

Franks, Violet "Gender and Psychotherapy" In *Gender and Disordered Behavior: Sex Differences in Psychopathology*. Edited by E.J. Gomberg, and V. Franks. New York: Brunner/Mazel, 1979.

Freedman, A.M., Kaplan, H.I., and Sadock, B.J. *Modern Synopsis of Comprehensive Textbook of Psychiatry*. Baltimore: Williams and Wilkins, 1972.

Garfinkel, P.E., and Garner, D.M. *Anorexia Nervosa*. New York: Brunner/Mazel, 1982.

Garner, D.M., Garfinkel, P.E., Schwartz, D., and Thompson, M. "Cultural Expectations of Thinness in Women." *Psychological Reports* 47(1980): 483-491.

Gilligan, C. *In a Different Voice: Psychological Theory and Women's Development*. Cambridge: Harvard University Press, 1982.

Goldstein, A.J. "Learning Theory Insufficiency in Understanding Agoraphobia—a Plea for Empiricism." In *Proceedings of the First Meeting of the European Association for Behavior Therapy and Behavior Modification*. Munich: Urban and Schwarzenburg, 1973.

Gonsiorek, John. *Observations on Male Victims and Same-Sex Involvement in Sexual Exploitations of Clients by Therapists*. Minneapolis: Walk-In Counseling Center, 1984.

Goode, S. Testimony submitted at the Michigan Women's Task Force Public Forum, Nov. 21, 1980.

Gove, W. "The Relationship Between Sex Roles, Mental Illness and Marital Status." *Social Forces* 51(1972): 34-44.

Gove, Walter R. "Sex Differences in the Epidemiology of Mental Disorder: Evidence and Explanations." In *Gender and Disordered Behavior*, pp. 23-68. Edited by E.S. Gomberg, and V. Franks. New York: Brunner/Mazel, 1979.

Gove, W.E., and Tudor, J. "Adult Sex Roles and Mental Illness." *American Journal of Sociology* 78(1973): 812-835.

Greenberg, R.P., Fisher, S., and Shapiro, J. "Sex Role Development and Response to Medication by Psychiatric In-Patients." *Psychological Reports* 33(1973): 675-677.

Grunebaum, Henry, Nadelson, Carol G., and Macht, Lee B. "Sexual Activity with the Psychiatrist: A District Branch Dilemma." Presented at the 129th Annual Meeting of the American Psychiatric Association, Miami, Florida, May, 1976.

Guttentag, Marcia. *Personality and Psychopathology*. New York: Academic Press, 1980.

Guttentag, Marcia et al. *The Mental Health of Women*. New York: Academic Press, 1980.

Halmi, K.A., Falk, J.R., and Schwartz, E. "Binge-Eating and Vomiting: A Survey of a College Population." *Psychological Medicine* 11(1981): 697-706.

Hare-Mustin, Rachel T. "An Appraisal of the Relationship Between Women and Psychotherapy—80 Years After the Case of Dora." *American Psychologist* 38(May, 1983): 593-601.

Hare-Mustin, Rachel T. "Ethical Considerations in the Use of Sexual Contact in Psychotherapy." *Psychotherapy: Theory, Research and Practice* 11(Winter, 1974): 308-310.

Holroyd, J., and Brodsky, A. "Psychologist Attitudes and Practices Regarding Erotic and Nonerotic Physical Contact with Patients." *American Psychologist* 32(October, 1977): 843-849.

Horowitz, A. "The Pathways into Psychiatric Treatment: Some Differences Between Men and Women." *Journal of Health and Social Behavior* 18(June 1977): 169-178.

Israel, Joan. "A Feminist Works with Non-Traditional Clients." *Smith College Journal-School of Social Work* 6(Summer, 1979): 20-22.

Jordan, J., Surrey, J., and Kaplan, A. *Women and Empathy*. Wellesley, Massachusetts: Stone Center Working Papers Series, 1982.

Jourard, S.M., and Secord, P.R. "Body-Cathexis and the Ideal Female Figure." *Journal of Abnormal and Social Psychology* 50(1955): 243-246.

Kardener, S.H., Fuller, M., and Mensch, I.N. "A Survey of Physicians' Attitudes and Practices Regarding Erotic and Nonerotic Physical Contact with Patients.'' *American Journal of Psychiatry* 130(October, 1973): 1077-1081.

Kendell, R.E. ''A New Look at Hysteria.'' In *Hysteria,* pp. 27-36. Edited by Alec Roy. Toronto: John Wiley and Sons, 1982.

Kendell, R.E., Hall, P.J., Harley, A., and Babigian, H.M. ''The Epidemiology of Anorexia Nervosa.'' *Psychological Medicine* 3(1973): 200-203.

Kirsch, B. *Consciousness-Raising Groups as Therapy for Women and Women in Therapy.* New York: Brunnel/Mazel, 1974.

Klerman, G.H., and Weissman, M.M. ''Depressions Among Women: Their Nature and Causes.'' In *The Mental Health of Women,* pp. 57-92. Edited by Marcia Guttentag, Susan Salasin, and Deborah Belle. New York: Academic Press, 1980.

Kravets, D. ''Sexism in a Woman's Profession.'' *Social Work* 21(Nov., 1976): 421-426.

Kravits, J., Anderson, R., and Anderson, O., eds. *Equity in Health Services: Empirical Analyses in Social Policy.* Cambridge, Massachusetts: Ballinger, 1975.

LaFarge, Phyllis. ''The New Woman.'' *Parent's Magazine,* October, 1983, pp. 84-156.

Lenane, K.J., and Lenane, R.J. ''Alleged Psychogenic Disorders in Women: A Possible Manifestation of Sexual Prejudice.'' *New England Journal of Medicine* 6(1973): 288-292.

Luepker, Ellen T., and Retsch-Bogart, Carol. ''Group Treatment for Clients Who Have Been Sexually Involved with Their Psychotherapists.'' Unpublished paper, 1980 (available from: Ellen Luepker, ACSW, Minneapolis Family and Children's Services, 414 South 8th Street, Minneapolis, Minnesota 55404).

MacKinnon, Roger A., and Michels, Robert, MD *The Psychiatric Interview in Clinical Practice.* Philadelphia: W.B. Saunders Co., 1971.

Maffeo, Patricia. ''Thoughts on Stricker's Implications of Research for Psychotherapeutic Treatment of Women.'' *American Psychologist* 34(August, 1979): 690-695.

Manheimer, D.E., Mellinger, G.D., and Balter, M.B. ''Psychotherapeutic Drugs: Use Among Adults in California.'' *California Medicare* 109(1968): 445-51.

Marazzi, Mary Ann. ''Anorexia Nervosa: An Anorexic Factor?'' Grant application to the Michigan Women's Task Force Public Forum, Dec. 12, 1980.

Marciniak, D. ''Stress Management for Low-Income Women.'' Testimony Submitted at the Michigan Women's Task Force Public Forum, Dec. 12, 1980.

Marks, I.M. ''Agoraphobic Syndrome (Phobic Anxiety State).'' *Archives of General Psychiatry* 23(1970): 538-553.

Mathews, A.M., Gelder, M.G., and Johnston, D.W. *Agoraphobia–Nature and Treatment.* New York: The Guilford Press, 1981.

Mayer, Jean, and Goldberg, Jeanne. ''Nutrition: The Binge Eating and Induced Vomiting of Bulimia Can Cause Tooth Decay, Potassium Loss, Kidney Damage and Death.'' *Detroit Free Press,* 13 May 1982, p. 30.

McManus, M., Alessi, N., and Grapentine, W.C. ''A Report to the State of Michigan: A Psychiatric Study of Adolescents in DMH Inpatient Facilities.'' Unpublished Report, The University of Michigan, Ann Arbor, Michigan, October 1982.

Mental Health and Aging Advisory Group. *Are They Worth It?* Lansing, Michigan: Office of Services to the Aging, 1980.

Milgrom, J. ''Some Observations Regarding Secondary Victims of Sexual Exploitation of Clients by Therapists and Counselors.'' Minneapolis: Walk-In Counseling Center, 1981.

Miller, J.B. *Toward a New Psychology of Women.* Boston: Beacon Press, 1976.

Miller, J.B. *Women and Power.* Wellesley, Massachusetts: Stone Center Working Papers Series, 1982.

Minuchin, S., Rosman, B.L., and Baker, L. *Psychosomatic Females: Anorexia Nervosa in Context.* Cambridge: Harvard University Press, 1978.

Money, J., and Erhardt, A.A. *Man and Woman: Boy and Girl.* Baltimore: Johns Hopkins Press, 1972.

Nadelson, T., and Eisenberg, L. ''The Successful Professional Woman: On Being Married to One.'' *The American Journal of Psychiatry* 134 (Oct., 1977): 1071-1076.

Naierman, Naomi et al. *Sex Discrimination in Health and Human Development Services.* Washington, D.C.: Abt Associates, 1979.

National Council of CMCH's Women's Task Force. *Women's Task Force Position Paper on Women's Service Issues.* Submitted at a Board Meeting of the National Council of CMH Centers, June, 1980.

Paffenbarger, R., and McCabe, L. "The Effects of Obstetric and Prenatal Events on Risk of Mental Illness in Women of Child-Bearing Age." *American Journal of Public Health* 56(1966): 400-407.

Parlee, M.B. "Comments on 'Roles of Activation and Inhibition in Sex Differences in Cognitive Abilities' by Broverman, Klaiber, Kobayshi, and Vogel." *Psychological Review* 79(1972): 180-184.

Parloff, M.B., Woskow, P.E., and Wolfe, B.E. "Research on Therapist Attitudes in Relation to Process and Outcome.: In *Handbook of Psychotherapy and Behavior Change.* Edited by S.L. Garfield, and A.E. Bergin. New York: Wiley, 1978.

Parry, H.J., Baltern, M.B., Mellinger, G.D., Cisin, I.H., and Manheimer, D.I. "National Patterns to Psychotherapeutic Drug Use." *Archives of General Psychiatry* 28(1973): 769-83.

Parry, Hugh J. "Patterns of Psychotropic Drug Use Among American Adults." *Journal of Drug Issues* 1(Oct., 1971): 269-273.

Paykel, E.S., Myers, J.K., Dienclt, M., Klerman, G.L., Lindethal, J.J., and Pepper, M.P. "Life Events and Depression: A Controlled Study." *Archives of General Psychiatry* 21(1969): 753-60.

Pearlin, L. "Sex Roles and Depression." In *Life Span Developmental Psychology: Normative Life Crises.* Edited by N. Datan and L. Ginsberg. New York: Academic Press, 1975.

President's Commission on Mental Health Report. Special Populations Subpanel on the Mental Health of Women, February 15, 1978.

Radov, C.G., Masnick, B.R., and Hauser, B.B. "Issues in Feminist Therapy: The Work of a Women's Study Group." *Social Work* 22(Nov., 1977): 507-509.

Rassieur, Charles L. *The Problem Clergymen Don't Talk About.* Philadelphia: Westminster Press, 1976.

Rich, A. *Of Woman Born: Motherhood as Experience and Institution.* New York: Bantam, 1970.

Robertson, J. "A Treatment Model for Post-Partum Depression." *Canada's Mental Health* 28(1980): 16-17.

Rosenthal, D. *Genetic Theory and Abnormal Behavior.* New York: McGraw-Hill, 1970.

Roy, Alec, ed. *Hysteria.* Toronto: John Wiley and Sons, 1982.

Rubin, L. *Women of a Certain Age.* New York: Harper and Row, 1979.

Russo, N.F., and Hilberman, E. *ERA: Psychological, Social and Ethical Implications for Psychology.* U.S. Educational Resources Information Center, (ED 169 397) Washington, D.C.: Sept., 1979.

Russo, N.F., and VandenBos, G.R. "Women in the Mental Health Delivery System." In *A Community Mental Health Sourcebook for Board and Professional Action.* Edited by W.H. Silverman. New York: Praeger, 1980.

Ryan, V. Testimony submitted at the Women's Task Force Public Forum, Feb. 20, 1981.

Schoener, Gary. "The Chronic Caller." *STASH Capsules* 6 (December, 1974).

Schoener, Gary. *Filing Complaints of Unethical or Unprofessional Conduct Against Counselors and Psychotherapists.* Revised ed. Minneapolis: Walk-In Counseling Center, 1979.

Schoener, Gary, Milgrom, Jeanette, and Gonsiorek, John. *Responding Therapeutically to Clients who have been Sexually Involved with their Psychotherapists.* Minneapolis: Walk-In Counseling Center, 1983.

Seiden, A.M. "Overview: Research on the Psychology of Women: II. Women in Families, Work, and Psychotherapy." *The American Journal of Psychotherapy* 133(1976): 1111-1123.

Selvini, Palazzoli, M.P. *Anorexia Nervosa.* London: Chanar, 1974.

Seniors and Substance Abuse Task Force. *Substance Abuse Among Michigan's Senior Citizens: Current Issues and Future Directions.* Lansing, Michigan: Michigan Office of Services to the Aging, 1978.

Serdenberg, Robert. "Images of Health, Illness and Women in Drug Advertising." *Journal of Drug Issues* 4(1974): 264-267.

Sheehy, Gail. "Pathfinders: Exploring the Road to Happiness." *Family Circle* February, 1982, pp. 43-46.

Sheehy, Gail. *Pathfinders.* New York: William Morrow, 1981.

Slater, E. "What is Hysteria?" In *Hysteria,* pp. 37-40. Edited by Alec Roy. Toronto: John Wiley and Sons, 1982.

Solomon, Z., and Bromet, E. "The Role of Social Factors in Affective Disorder: An Assessment of the Vulnerability Model of Brown and His Colleagues." *Psychological Medicine* 12(1982): 123.

Sommer, B. "The Effect of Menstruation on Cognitive and Perceptual-Motor Behavior: A Review." *Psychosomatic Medicine* 35(1973): 515-534.

Stephenson, Susan, and Walker, Lillian. "Psychotropic Drugs and Women." *Bioethics Quarterly* 2(Spring, 1980).

Stiver, I. *Work Inhibitions in Women.* Wellesley, Massachusetts: Stone Center Working Papers Series, 1982.

Sundstrom, Ingrid. "Sex and the Therapist." *Mpls.,* October 1977, pp. 39-41, 79-80, 82-83.

Test, M.A., and Berlin, S.B. "Issues of Special Concern to Chronically Mentally Ill Women." *Professional Psychology* 12(February, 1981): 136-145.

Thorne, B. and Yalom, M. eds. *Rethinking the Family: Some Feminist Questions.* New York: Longman, 1982.

Thorne, B., Kramarae, C., and Henley, N. "Language, Gender and Society: Opening a Second Decade of Research." In *Language, Gender and Society,* pp. 7-24. Edited by B. Thorne, C. Kramarae, and N. Henley. Rowley, Massachusetts: Newbury House, 1983.

Thorne, Barrie. "A Perspective on Women's Mental Health Problems." Testimony submitted to the Michigan Women's Task Force, Lansing, Michigan, September 19, 1980.

Tourre, D. Testimony submitted at the Michigan Women's Task Force Public Forum, June 19, 1981.

U.S. Department of Health, Education and Welfare. *Elderly and Psychoactive Drugs.* Washington, D.C.: U.S. Department of Health, Education and Welfare, 1979.

Veroff, J., Douvan, E., and Kulka, R.A. *The Inner American.* New York: Basic Books, 1981.

Wahl, O.F. "Monozygotic Twins Discordant for Schizophrenia: A Review." *Psychological Bulletin* 83(1976): 91-106.

Weintraub, M.I. *Hysterical Conversion Reactions.* Jamaica, N.Y.: Spectrum, 1983.

Weissman, M., and Klerman, G.L. "Sex Differences and the Epidemiology of Depression." *Archives of General Psychiatry* 34(1977): 98-111.

Weissman, M.M., and Klerman, G.L. "Sex Differences and the Epidemiology of Depression." In *Gender and Disordered Behavior,* pp. 381-425. Edited by E.S. Gomberg and V. Franks. New York: Brunner/Mazel, 1979.

West, C., and Zimmerman, D. "Small Insults: A Study of Interruptions in Cross-Sex Conversations Between Unacquainted Persons." In *Language, Gender and Society,* pp. 96-111. Edited by B. Thorne, C. Kramarae, and N. Henley. Rowley, Massachusetts: Newbury House, 1983.

Woodruff, R.A., Goodwin, D.W., and Guze, S.B. "Hysteria (Briquet's Syndrome)." In *Hysteria,* pp. 117-129. Edited by Alec Roy. Toronto: John Wiley and Sons, 1982.

Wright, Ann. (Personal Communication) 1980.

Zola, I. "Culture and Symptoms: An Analysis of Patients' Pressing Complaints." *American Sociological Review* 31(1966): 615-630.